Jesus and Paul

JESUS

SIGNS OF

Wilfrid

Michael Glazier

PAUL AND CONTRADICTION

Harrington, O.P.

Wilmington   Delaware

WILFRID HARRINGTON, O.P., a graduate of the University of St. Thomas, Rome, and École Biblique, Jerusalem, is Professor of Scripture at the Milltown Institute of Theology and Philosophy and the Dominican House of Studies, Dublin. He has lectured in the U.S.A. and Great Britain, Australia, New Zealand, India, and West Indies. Published works include: *Key to the Bible* (3 vols.), *Understanding the Apocalypse, Parables Told by Jesus, The Path of Biblical Theology, Christ and Life, Spirit of the Living God, The New Guide to Reading and Studying the Bible,* and *Mark* (Volume 4 of the *New Testament Message* series).

First published in 1987 by Michael Glazier, Inc., 1935 West Fourth Street, Wilmington, Delaware 19805. ©Copyright 1987 by Michael Glazier, Inc. All rights reserved. Library of Congress Catalog Card Number: 86-45322. International Standard Book Number: 0-89453-591-9.
Printed in the United States of America.

IN MEMORY OF
PAUL HYNES
DOMINICAN
A MAN OF
FAITH • VISION • COURAGE

CONTENTS

— *This child is set . . . for a sign of contradiction* (Lk 2:34).

— *We are fools for Christ's sake* (1 Cor 4:10).

PROLOGUE

We cannot but believe that the first Christians had an
understanding of Jesus sharpened by their very nearness to
"the things that have happened in these days...concerning
Jesus of Nazareth" (Lk 24:18–19)...an understanding that,
for us, has become blurred not only by time but by centuries
of christian division and, let it be honestly said, by an
oppressive weight of theology. It is not easy for us to fight
our way through to Jesus of Nazareth. It is essential that we
strive. It goes without saying that our quest of Jesus will not
be wholly successful. But the quest itself is a liberating
experience. We will quickly learn, as we take our first steps
on the way, that we cannot hope to get far unless we shed
excess baggage: the inhibitions loaded on us and the mistaken
ideas we carry.

We do want to make our way to God. What we must learn
to accept is that God has first made his way to us! The
original sin was man's snatching at the wisdom that could
only be his as gift (Gen 3:1–7). Humanity's sin continues to
be its striving to escape the ways of God. It has long perplexed and disturbed me that Old Testament men and

women often have had a deeper understanding of God and, certainly, a more personal relationship with God than is the experience of many Christians. In Jesus of Nazareth the divine has entered into our world, our history; God has become one of us. But we would bypass the way of God. That primal temptation is still there: "you will be like God." The basic christian truth is: "I am the way" (Jn 14:6). If God's way to humankind is through the man Jesus, then our way to God is through the man Jesus.

Jesus

I have stressed the man Jesus — is Jesus not God? I would suggest that the statement "Jesus is God" is not only not a criterion of orthodoxy; I would argue that it effectively blunts the challenge of Jesus. A Jesus who is "God" is a Jesus whom we can manipulate — we can make anything we please of "God." Besides, to say "Jesus is God" implies not only that we know who Jesus is — but that we know who and what God is. The great medieval theologians had the wisdom to know that they did not know God — their *via negativa* declared that one knows about God only what he is not.

Jesus, the man of flesh and blood, we cannot manipulate. He is an uncomfortable person to have around. And he shows us the true visage of God, whom we find to be, paradoxically, a *Deus humanissimus* — a supremely human God — this Father of our Lord Jesus Christ. But we can see him only if we allow Jesus of Nazareth to be human. Let me make myself clear. I assert, with total conviction, that in the man

Jesus I meet my God. I stake my life on the truth that the man Jesus is Emmanuel, that he is God-with-us. We are faced with mystery here. And how is one to speak of this unique meeting of God with humankind in terms that will not betray one or other aspect of the mystery? For my part, I am not prepared to sacrifice Jesus' humanness to a misguided concern to "rescue" his divinity.

Paul assures us that "God was in Christ, reconciling the world to himself" (2 Cor 5:19). My God, then, is a God bent on humankind. My God is a God who so loves this human world that he gave his Son (Jn 3:16). My God acknowledges the worship of him in his children's caring for one another. That is what the great prophets of Israel saw and taught. That is the way and the message of Jesus of Nazareth. Truly our God is not like other gods. Our God is not preoccupied with his dignity but is wholly concerned with our good. But we seek a God in our image. We want God to be God — for heaven's sake! Deep down we are, like Peter, scandalized by the folly of the cross (Mk 8:31-33). A God whose divine respect for his human creature is such that he gives his Son is too much for us. We are, basically, snobs. I want to relate to my God on an I-Thou basis; I want my God to pay attention to me. I do not like to be told that the meeting-place with God is the sacrament of my brother and sister. Will the elder son in the parable of the Prodigal Son acknowledge his brother and enter into the joy of his return (Lk 15:31-32)? Only so can he know his Father as father. We may ignore, but we cannot deny, that such is the praxis and the teaching of Jesus (cf Mt 25:31-46).

This Tremendous Lover

The grace of my life has been the study of Scripture. Towards the end of three decades of teaching a pattern emerges, starkly: The Bible is nothing other than the turbulent love-story of God and humankind. *This Tremendous Lover* is the title of a book on prayer by the Irish Cistercian, Eugene Boylan, an inspired title which aptly describes our God. This Tremendous Lover — too big for our pettiness. We are adept at cutting God to our measure. Happily, our paper-patterns will never translate into anything real. God, gently or painfully, sets our ways aside. He is the Father who really knows what is best for his children. Why, then, does he let us hurt ourselves and hurt one another so? I have come to understand that God, our Father, has infinite respect for us. He is a God of power, omnipotent — but he is never a God of force. His respect for his creatures, above all for his human creatures, is divine. He invites us, longingly, lovingly, to respect one another. The temptation is to look through our human chaos to an uncaring God. The challenge is to find, in our troubled world, the presence of a loving God. If true love respects the one loved, what can we expect of a loving God? One needs humility (another word for honesty) to learn the reality of love.

It is a wondrous and humbling thought that God has such respect for us. If we would grasp this truth, so much would hang together. There is, in all of us, something of the impatience of the Pharisees who sought a sign from heaven (Mk 8:11). We will not be content with the human way. Someone has said that the secret of holiness is the doing of ordinary things extraordinarily well. Jesus went about "doing good." There is little doubt that his way was far less marked by the miraculous than the gospels would suggest. We have come to realize the extent to which the Jesus-story has been colored by Easter-faith. In the light of their encounter with the risen Lord there is no way that the disciples could ever again think of Jesus only as they had known him before his death. What is encouraging is that the pre-Easter Jesus of Nazareth is still so accessible to us.

Paul

Often enough, in the past, it was fashionable to set Jesus and Paul in opposition. Jesus' message was all light and sweetness. Paul struck a harsh note, especially with his grim theology of the cross. It was obvious that he had never understood Jesus and had, in effect, perverted the gospel of Jesus. It might seem that I am being simplistic; in fact it would not be difficult to adduce scholarly support of such a view. Yet, today, we see how very wide of the mark it was. For my part, I become more and more convinced that no one has ever understood Jesus as well as Paul has. I have described him as "the exegete of Jesus" and so I firmly regard him.

What I seek to do in this book is something quite straightforward: firstly, to look at Jesus — his person and message — and then to see how well Paul has assimilated and presented that person and that message. To find Jesus one must go behind the gospels. I am not suggesting that the evangelists have given us a false picture — anything but that. But, because they have written in the full light of their

Easter faith, inevitably, the Jesus they project is larger than life. In that, of course, they are quite right because Jesus is larger than life. At the same time they have, inevitably also, distorted something of the impact he made on his contemporaries. Already in the gospels we find a tendency that has plagued Christianity ever since: the tendency to stress the otherworldliness of Jesus Christ at the cost of his humanness. It seems to me that, among the evangelists, Mark has been least affected by the tendency. Consequently, Mark will be my main source in my reach to the "historical Jesus."

A Servant of Jesus Christ

That brings me back to Paul — for Mark and Paul have in common a striking theological emphasis: a *theologia crucis* — a theology of the cross. And this leads to a proper perspective on our study. I do not want to give the impression that what only matters for Christians and for christian living is a looking to the historical Jesus and a being guided by him. I certainly do not seek to ignore the fact that what galvanized the faith of the first Christians was the conviction that the crucified Jesus had been raised from the dead and exalted to the Father. No one was more emphatic than Paul that a "good news" without the proclamation of Jesus risen and exalted could not be the christian gospel (cf 1 Cor 15:14-19). My bringing in of Paul surely saves me from a charge of reductionism. My contention is that Paul, who had never known Jesus of Nazareth in the flesh, had grasped that the word of his risen Lord was word of that Jesus of flesh and blood.

I do not invoke Paul to cover myself. My point is that he does reach, behind the Christ Jesus of his confession, the man Jesus of Nazareth. Paul is a man obsessed: "to me, to live is Christ" (Phil 1:21). Still, from Paul's letters, one might get the impression that the earthly life of Jesus was of no great interest to him. But then, these letters are "occasional," dealing with specific situations and problems. They cannot be expected to give us more than an odd glimpse of Paul's own telling of the Jesus' story. We have a precious pointer to the fact that Paul did know the story. He informs us that, three years after his traumatic experience on the Damascus road, he "went to Jerusalem to visit Cephas and remained with him fifteen days" (Gal 1:18). When he adds, "I saw none of the other apostles except James the Lord's brother" (v.19), one gets the impression that Paul and Peter were in conclave for a fortnight. Can we doubt that, for both of them, Jesus must have been the dominant theme of their conversation? Knowing Paul as we do from his letters one imagines that Peter must have felt like a wet rag at the end of the session. Paul would have been avid in his seeking for information about this Jesus. And who, better than Peter, could have met his need? James, too, would have made his contribution. This may well have been the most important two weeks in the life of Paul. Given his wholehearted commitment to Jesus Christ, one may reasonably postulate that Paul of Tarsus was uncommonly well-informed about the life of Jesus of Nazareth.

I aim to let Jesus and Paul speak for themselves. The size of the book is sufficient indication that my goal is modest —one does not find here the whole Jesus nor the whole Paul. What I do want to stress is the challenge of the persons and the message of Master and Disciple. It will be found that there is a parallel, not contrived, between the corresponding chapters, (for instance, Four and Eleven), of the two parts of the book — a feature which serves to underline their common thrust. Jesus and Paul were "signs of contradiction" (cf Lk 2:34) in their own day. My contention is that it is a sign of health still to see them so. A singular and tragic achievement of historical Christianity has been the effective domestication of Jesus and of Paul.

I

JESUS

1

WHO DO YOU SAY THAT I AM?

The voice of prophecy had been still for centuries. The Jewish people had grown used to looking only to the ritual of the priesthood and the teaching of the scribes. Now, however, they flocked to the Jordan, drawn there by a strange man of rude appearance and stern words. What he had to say was not comforting, but it was compelling. He called for nothing less than a radical change of heart — *metanoia*. And his water baptism was a seal upon repentance. One day a young man who had journeyed from Nazareth of Galilee, stepped forward to be baptized. Jesus had heard of John and had come to see for himself. He liked what he saw and heard. John the Baptist was the only person in the society of his day who impressed Jesus. He shared with John an awareness of Damocles' sword, of the catastrophe, that threatened Israel. Their nation was bent on conflict with Rome. The result could but be disaster.

Though he admired John, Jesus followed his own way. John was a prophet of doom who preached a "baptism of repentance for the forgiveness of sins" (Mk 1:4). Jesus proclaimed: "the kingdom of God is at hand" (1:15). Where John prophesied the judgment of God, Jesus prophesied the salvation of God. Hearing, in prison, of the activity of Jesus, a perplexed John sent two of his disciples to enquire: "Are you he who is to come, or shall we look for another?" (Lk 7:19). And the answer was: "Go and tell John what you have seen and heard: the blind receive their sight, the lame walk, lepers are cleansed, and the deaf hear, the dead are raised up, the poor have the good news preached to them" (7:22). There is another prophetic message, another prophetic style. Jesus declared that the catastrophe was not inevitable. If there were a change of heart the kingdom would come, not the catastrophe. In any event it was the catastrophe (the disastrous Jewish-Roman war of 66-70 A.D.) that happened.

Who Do You Say That I Am?

At a turning-point in his gospel, credibly reflecting a turning-point in the ministry of Jesus, Mark has Jesus ask his disciples: "Who do you say that I am?" (Mk 8:29). Reminiscence of an historical moment it seems to be, but the handling of it by the evangelists differs notably from gospel to gospel. In Mark, Peter gives the straightforward reply: "You are the Christ (Messiah)" and then goes on to demonstrate that he has a wholly mistaken notion of the nature of that Messiahship (8:29-33). In Matthew Peter's answer is the solemn: "You are the Christ, the Son of the living God" (Mt 16:16) — a fulsome christian profession of faith. In Luke the setting of the episode is indeterminate (the others site it at Caesasea Philippi); the reply is "the Christ of God" and there is no rebuke by or of Peter (Lk 9:20-22).

These differences are not negligible. What is of interest, though, is that even Luke has Jesus spell out his own understanding of Messiahship: "The Son of man must suffer many things, and be rejected by the elders and chief priests and scribes, and be killed, and on the third day be raised" (Lk 9:22). This is the first of the "three predictions of the passion" (Mk 8:31; 9:31; 10:33-34, parr.) As they stand, these predictions are, unquestionably, *vaticinia ex eventu*. It is not, however, surprising that, towards the end, Jesus should have foreseen the likelihood, the probability indeed, of a violent death. For that matter, at Gethsemane, he was faced with a painful decision. He had preached the rule of God, had striven to make it a reality. It must have seemed to him that his mission faced the ultimate frustration: his prophetic voice would be stilled in death.

"Who do you say that I am?" That question is asked of each christian generation. That question is addressed to every Christian. It is salutary to recall that the first answer to the question, while seemingly right, was, in reality, wide of the mark. Peter was not the first disciple, nor the last, whose understanding of Jesus does not match the titles so easily bestowed. In this chapter, I shall look at the man Christ Jesus as we may glimpse him through the gospels. And then I shall indicate how christology today is coming to terms with the past. It seems to be that we have reached a more uncluttered view of Jesus and a clearer understanding of the God of Jesus.

Mark

Though there are some voices of dissent, the overwhelming consensus of scholarly opinion is that Mark is our earliest gospel. I find the contention that Mark is based on Matthew and Luke to be, frankly, incredible. A case of sorts can be made (and has been made) for this position on the basis of a comparative study of synoptic passages. But once Mark is treated as a literary unit its sturdy independence is compelling. By the same token, acknowledgment of the evangelist's creative role further underlines the theological dimension of his gospel. The fact that Mark has to contend with a flawed christology and, as a corrective, must strive to present a truer understanding of Jesus, gives hope that, across his pages, we may get as close as one could expect to the historical Jesus.

The evangelist's chief problem seems to have been that some of his community wanted their Christianity without the cross. Throughout the gospel all humans — the Twelve most of all — fail to understand who Jesus is. Strangely, the "unclean spirits" do know him; but they are bound to silence. The sole voice of authentic confession is that of the centurion. He had witnessed the death of Jesus and, as he gazed on that corpse hanging on the cross, declared in awe: "Truly, this man was the Son of God?" (15:39). The whole tenor of his gospel, culminating in this dramatic scene, is Mark's powerful way of declaring that no one can understand Jesus, no one can truly confess him, who has not come to terms with the cross. It appears to me, then, that as well, if not better, than any other, Mark has, in his gospel, given an apt answer to the question: "Who do you say that I am?" We would see something of the Jesus who emerges.

Son of God and Son of Man

Mark opens his gospel with the headline: "The beginning of the gospel of Jesus Christ, the Son of God" (1:1). The title, we have noted, is caught up in the climactic confession of the centurion. It is a title acknowledged by Jesus himself when solemnly challenged by the high priest: "Are you the Christ, the Son of the Blessed (i.e. the Son of God)?" And Jesus said, "I am" (14:61-62). Jesus was formally addressed as "my beloved Son" by the heavenly voice at Baptism and Transfiguration (1:11; 9:7). Time and again the unclean spirits voice their recognition of him. It is enough to note the summary statement: "And whenever the unclean spirits beheld him, they fell down before him and cried out, 'You are the Son of God'," (3:11). Then there is the title: Son of man. The Son of man has authority on earth to forgive sins (2:10), he is lord even of the Sabbath (2:28). He is one who will sit at the right hand of God (15:62) and will come on the clouds to gather his elect (13:26-27). Besides, Jesus has power over evil spirits and over nature (6:45-52). And, as for teaching: "What is this? A new teaching with authority behind it" (1:27).

All of this is the christology of the early church (and of Mark). That christology was not built on air. There was something very striking about Jesus; he had a mysterious dimension to him. Jesus appears as very much a man in our world. And yet he was a man not fully at home in our world. The gospels, of course, reflect the light of resurrection-faith. Yet, even when we have filtered out that light, as much as ever is possible, we are still left with a Jesus who is larger than life. Take the call of the disciples. The account of it (for instance, Mk 1:16-20; 2:13-14) is obviously stylized. Still, there is the recollection of extraordinary magnetism. Only the final disaster shook the confidence of the eleven. (We do not know when or why Judas began to waver.) It is helpful to look more closely at the titles. We begin, not with a title bestowed on Jesus, but with Jesus' own title for his God.

Abba

Jesus was one who had a serene relationship with God. Without any self-consciousness he spoke of "Father" and "Son"; he turned with simple confidence to that Father in prayer. The gospel evidence points to Jesus' consistent use of the term *Abba* in speaking of God, and especially in prayer to God. Admittedly, in the gospels, the Aramaic word is met with only once (Mk 14:36) — not surprisingly in documents written in Greek. But the term stands behind "the Father," "Father" or "my father" in all strands of the gospel tradition. Abba, originally an infant-word, was, in Jesus' day, a familiar designation of one's earthly father; it carried a connotation of tenderness but also implied a recognition of benign authority. That Jesus regularly addressed his God as Abba shows his unconventional regard towards and intimate communion with God. Because he really knew his God he could dare to call him Abba. Still, his use of the intimate "Abba" does not seem to have shocked his friends. They appear to have taken his mode of address in their stride and felt encouraged to address their God in the same manner as he. This is clearly present in Luke's version of the Lord's Prayer: "When you pray, say: Father (i.e. Abba)" (11:1-2).

That early Christians did pray so we know from Galatians 4:6 and Romans 3:15 (the only places in the New Testament, apart from Mark 14:36, where the Aramaic word appears). Evidently, they did not regard Jesus' use of the term as pointing to the uniqueness of his sonship — otherwise they could never have addressed the Father in the same manner as he. What does follow is that they, rightly, recognized in Jesus' use of the title evidence of his religious experience of deep intimacy with God. They recognized that he knew God as no one ever before had known him. And if indeed Jesus had taught his disciples to pray in the same manner as he, it was precisely his disciples whom he so taught. For that matter, it is, Paul tells us, the Spirit of the Son sent by God into the heart of the Christian who cries "Abba."

It is significant that Jesus addressed his God as Abba in prayer. Jesus prayed because prayer is a feature of our human condition. His God was the Creator, the Sustainer of all. Jesus was wholly dependent on his God. He turned, spontaneously, to a Father who would support him, who would back him in his endeavours. True, he was one sent, one who had to plow his own furrow. But he was not alone, because the Father was with him. The prayer of Jesus, by example and not by contrived design, is meant to alert the disciple to his or her dependence on God. If the Son found a need and a joy in converse with his Father he could expect that the other children of God, his sisters and brothers, would also experience that want and that happiness.

Son

But back to Abba. If Jesus could consistently address his God with the unconventional title Abba, that surely says something of God and of their mutual relationship. We must look to Jesus' sense of sonship. Did Jesus think of himself as the Son? A key text is Matthew 11:27 —

> All things have been delivered to me by my Father; and no one knows the Son except the Father, and no one knows the Father except the Son and anyone to whom the Son chooses to reveal him (cf Lk 10:22).

This Johannine-sounding text is particularly interesting because it turns up both in Matthew and in Luke (it is, of course, a Q-saying). The question is, could Jesus have spoken of his relationship with God in such an absolute and exclusive manner? We have observed that Jesus prayed to God as Father. Here he claims to know God. One must recall that, in a Hebrew context, to speak of knowledge in a setting of personal relationships is to imply intimate relationship. In God-man relationship it describes the love and surrender stirred by the gracious love of God. It is the same I-Thou relationship expressed by Abba. Jesus relates to God with the warmth and intimacy of a son towards his father. We might note that the "all things" are the "these things" which the Father had hidden from the learned and the wise (v. 25). Jesus lays claim to a divinely-granted knowledge of God on which he bases the understanding of his mission.

Where should one seek the ground of Jesus' Abba-experience? I would answer: nowhere else than in his crea-turely status as a human being. It is true that he finds the center of his life in God — but that does not situate the center outside himself. Every human person is wholly dependent on God — but that can never result in a loss of humanness.[1] It is unfortunate that we think of incarnation in terms of two components: humanity and divinity. We should think of it as having two "aspects": a real humanity in which the "being of God" is realized.

It seems to me that the matter may be put even more forcefully. Another view is that the eternal and self-sufficient God freely and from eternity wills to be for another: he looks for a personal counterpart. In pursuance of this desire, God summoned forth the human race and, one day, out of that race which looked in hope to something beyond itself, came one who would be like him and who would respond to him wholly. In Jesus of Nazareth God met his own counterpart, the image and likeness of himself. To Jesus he could say, "My Son" and hear the spontaneous response, "Abba." Jesus was the answer to God's eternal decision not to be alone. In Johannine language, the Word became flesh and dwelt among us. For what is *Logos,* "Word," but God as he is communicable, as he can "converse" with humankind? The statement, "the Word was made flesh," can only mean that, in Jesus of Nazareth, we encounter God as fully as we can meet him. Paul, as one would expect, has got it exactly right: "God was in Christ ..." (2 Cor 5:19).

So much for God's resolve; what then of Jesus?

> Jesus achieves the fullness of personal growth, the full power of human personality, in confrontation and dialogue with the

---

[1] Edward Schillebeeckx, *Jesus. An Experiment in Christology* (New York: Crossroad, 1981, 256-271).

infinite mystery, the infinite person, who has no beginning and no end. Jesus becomes a person in the full and final sense in the encounter with God. Jesus is not merely a human being of whom God approves. He is one who becomes irrevocably himself in knowing and loving God — in being able to say "Father" to him.[2]

That way of putting it certainly underlines the humanness of Jesus. And, if anything has come through to me in my years of New Testament study, it is that Jesus of Nazareth, while surely more than human, is wholly human. Jesus was a human person while being, of course, unique in his human personality. Happily, today, theologians more and more declare as much — and without subtle qualification.

Son of God

The question still remains: What does Jesus imply by referring to God as his Abba? "Our Father" never occurs in the gospels as a personal address of Jesus — the "Our Father" of Matthew 6:9 is in a prayer meant for the disciples. It would seem that Jesus was conscious of a degree of distinctiveness in his relationship with God over against that of his disciples. The "my Father" "your Father" distinction is an expression of Jesus' self-awareness. He is the one who responds to God's address: "my Son." Jesus' sense of being God's Son was not only an intellectual belief, it was an existential conviction. He experienced a relationship of

[2]John C. Dwyer, *Son of Man and Son of God* (New York: Paulist, 1983, 129-130).

sonship. While he knew himself to be dependent on God he lived in such intimacy with God that the only words to describe their relationship were "Father" and "Son." At the same time, the synoptic evidence will not permit us to speak of something like Jesus' "divine consciousness." Simply, Jesus the man of Nazareth was conscious of a unique relationship to God. What really matters is that he was, in his human person and in his human life the revelation of that divine Father.

Son of Man

While "Son of man" carries emphatically christological overtones in our gospels, it is becoming increasingly accepted that Jesus did not speak of himself as Son of man in any theological sense. Among the arguments in favour of this view the most compelling might well be that Jesus did not need to explain to himself who he was. He was Son, and that is all there was to it. Nor did he seek to spell out for his disciples, not even for the Twelve, who he was. They would come to know him from his presence, his deeds, his words. He gave himself no titles nor claimed any. His Caesarea Philippi question was a challenge. As it turned out, the answer was hopelessly wide of the mark. What Peter understood by "Messiah" did not at all describe who Jesus was. It has not been easy, then or now, to say who Jesus is. Christology has done its best — and its less than best. It may be unhelpful and can be dangerous to attempt to define theoretically the mysterious nature of Jesus. "To attempt to define Jesus' nature is to limit it, to narrow it down, to bring it to a point that may well be too sharp, with the result that Jesus is either underestimated or overestimated."[3]

[3]Edward Schillebeeckx, *God is New Each Moment* (New York: The Seabury Press, 1983, 41).

2

THE RULE OF GOD

Jesus came into Galilee preaching the kingdom of God and saying, "The time is fulfilled and the kingdom of God is at hand" (Mk 1:14-15).

Jesus proclaimed the *basileia*, the rule of God. In the Jewish world of his day there was intense yearning for the "kingdom of God" — a kingdom that was diversely understood by different groups. In general, one might say that the vision which fueled expectation was of Israel as a "kingdom of priests and a holy nation" (Ex 19:6). And the conviction was that God's intervention on behalf of his people could be prepared for and hastened by their efforts to become the kingly and priestly people of God. In the main it was believed that the desired result could be achieved by faithful observance of Torah and through the Temple cult. The various groups within Judaism each had its own manner of hastening the coming of the kingdom. Thus, the Pharisees relied mainly on meticulous observance of Torah; the Essenes of Qumran, though they had distanced themselves from the official priesthood (in their book on illegitimate priesthood), saw themselves as the priestly elect of the nation; the Zealots would defend the Law and traditions with the sword.

In the midst of this diverse concern for the renewal of the people of Israel as God's holy elect stood Jesus who shared that concern. But he would not define the holiness of God's people in cultic terms. He redefined it in terms of wholeness. And where all other groups were, in their various ways, exclusive, the Jesus movement was inclusive. His challenge, and his invitation were to all.

Being Human

Jesus could declare that the rule of God was "at hand." It was already in the midst of his hearers — meaning that it was present in the person of Jesus himself. It has been a dominant christian tendency to project the kingdom wholly into the future; for that matter to make it a heavenly reality. This was surely not the view of Jesus. For him the rule of God has to be a reality among men and women here on earth. Of course, the kingdom which would emerge if God's rule were to hold sway would be very different from any existing political entity and different, too, from religious structures then and since. The theologians of liberation have got it right.

God's rule becomes real only when it finds expression in human lives. It found expression in the life of Jesus. He "went about, doing good"; he championed the outcast, he welcomed and pardoned sinners. Jesus, in his own life-style gave concrete expression to the good life — a life worthy of humankind. It is up to us, his disciples, in our different and greatly changed world to give expression — in our turn — to the good life. He demonstrated that the kingdom is a reality of this world. It is our task to give it flesh and blood in our world. This we can achieve by imitation of Christ — as Paul understood it. Not a vain attempt to be another Jesus; he, like every human being, is unique. We "imitate Christ" by being our authentic selves, by activating our human potential. And this we achieve in the same fashion as he: by openness to the Abba and his purpose. This is what salvation is all about: that we become fully human. And that means humanness as Jesus lived it.

Defining God

The kingdom can be a reality only at the cost of wholehearted conversion. That is why the demands of Jesus are so uncompromising. He knew, better than any other, that sin is the greatest evil, the ultimate slavery. But he discerned sin in structures and selfishness, in privilege and greed. He took his stand on the Fatherhood (Motherhood) of God. He firmly believed that all men and women are children of that Father/Mother, that all are sisters and brothers. That is why he could demand: "Love your enemy" —because the "enemy" is my brother or sister! He regarded sin as whatever conflicts with that family relationship of respect and love. Logically, then, his message is "good news for the poor." The poor are victims of the oppressive power of sin, an oppression mediated through sinful structures.

Jesus' "beatitudes" are prophecy. I speak of *his* beatitudes (accurately caught by Luke): "Blessed are you poor — blessed are you that hunger now — blessed are you that weep now" (Lk 6:20-21). He assures the poor that theirs is the kingdom of God. For, if his preaching were to bring about the desired change of heart, they would come into their own. At this stage in his ministry he confidently expected that the hoped-for radical renewal of Israel would occur. Matthew, we know, later "spiritualized" the beatitudes. Jesus was more realistic — and thereby more idealistic.

In preaching the rule of God Jesus was defining God. He was proclaiming a God bent on the salvation of humankind. That is why he announced good news to the poor — the needy of every sort, the outcast. That is why he was friend of sinners, why he had tablefellowship with them. And, in the long run, it was because Jesus had preached a God of overwhelming mercy that he ended up on a cross. That God was unacceptable to the religious people of his day. That God is unacceptable to the professional religious of any day.

In only two places in the synoptic gospels (Mk 12:33; Lk 11:42) is there word of our love for God, and it appears sparingly in the rest of the New Testament. Usually, the emphasis is on God's love for humankind. And this is as it should be. It is because God has first loved us that we love God (Rom 5:5,8; 1 Jn 4:11). Jesus himself showed in his life and death the quality of this twofold love. His love for God motivated his total dedication to his mission; his love for men and women marked him as one who would lay down his life as a ransom for humankind (Mk 10:45).

The Friend of Sinners

A man apart, and yet a man touching the hearts of people. He was at home with the simple folk who clearly felt at ease with him. He was a friend of sinners. The designation "sinners" could cover all who did not live by the standards of meticulous pharisaic observance. Such were outcasts, beyond God's concern: "This rabble, who do not know the law, are accursed" (Jn 7:49). But sinners were also those who knew their need, their unworthiness before God. Jesus was their friend. And we must not be tempted to suppose that they were repentant sinners before he befriended them. No, Jesus met them in their brokenness. Of course, they responded. "Go and sin no more" — Jesus was not indifferent to sin; he was indifferent to the sinful past of people who came to him. He knew that God's forgiveness is total. We can readily shield ourselves from the implications of Jesus' deed and teaching.

Jesus reveals God as a God bent on humankind. Jesus' God is indifferent to what men and women might do to him. He is supremely concerned over what we do or might do to one another. Paul, as usual, had got it right: "For the whole law is fulfilled in one word, 'You shall love your neighbour as yourself'" (Gal 5:14; cf Rom 13:8-10). This, too, is the drift of Matthew's "judgment-scene" (Mt 25:31-46). God is pleading with us to be his children. It is God who will bring about his rule ("thy kingdom come" = "establish your rule").

But God, with his unflinching respect for human freedom, will not compel us. It is only by our letting God be God that the kingdom will come. And that can only be through our treating one another as brothers and sisters within the love-motivated family he wants us to be.

Jesus first proclaimed the rule of God not in words but in his own person and through his own life-style. Because the followng chapters will reveal aspects of his proclamation, it is not necessary here, to go into further detail. It is important only to stress that Jesus proclaimed God as a caring God. The God of Jesus may be king — but he is like no earthly king. That is the burden of the declaration of the Johannine Jesus: "My kingship is not of this world" (Jn 18:36). The kingdom of God is not and will not be a kingdom measured by the standards of the world. It is a kingdom that turns worldly standards upside down.

> The kingdom in which Jesus wants his contemporaries to believe was a kingdom of love and service, a kingdom of human brotherhood in which every man is loved and respected because he is a man. Nobody can believe in and hope for such a kingdom unless he has learned to be moved with compassion for his fellow-man. God has now revealed himself as the God of compassion. His power is the power of compassion. Man's compassion for man releases God's power into the world, the only power that can bring about the miracle of the kingdom.[1]

[1]Albert Nolan, *Jesus Before Christianity* (New York: Orbis Books, 1978, 84).

When one looks back on the nearly twenty centuries of Christianity, one may be hard put to recognize features of that kingdom in the ecclesiastical empire. One has to search for compassion behind the borrowed trappings of Caesar. "It shall not be so among you . . .".

3

COME TO SERVE

Luke has Jesus open his ministry in the Nazareth synagogue. Historical or not, it is an appropriate setting and the Isaian text which he chose certainly mapped the program which he was to follow:

> The Spirit of the Lord is upon me, because he has anointed me to preach good news to the poor. He has sent me to proclaim release to the captives and recovering of sight to the blind, to set at liberty those who are oppressed, to proclaim the acceptable year of the Lord (Lk 4:18-19; cf Is 61:1-2).

Later, when a perplexed Baptist sent two of his disciples to Jesus to learn if he really were the "one to come," the prophet of the end-time, they were told: "Go and tell John what you have seen and heard: the blind receive their sight, the lame walk, lepers are cleansed, and the deaf hear, the dead are raised up, the poor have the good news preached to them" (Lk 7:22).

Jesus' mission was firmly political — by the very fact that it was conventionally apolitical. He did not side with any party. Inevitably, his "preferential option for the poor" brought him into conflict with the establishment of church and state. If Jesus' preaching of "good news to the poor" displayed a preference for the needy and the outcast it was not an exclusive option. Rather, for him "poor" embraced the whole of humanity; those most in need were those who did not know their need. Jesus did not avoid his opponents; he dialogued with them. It is striking that so many of his extant parables are addressed to his opponents. True, he is critical of them, of their tragic misunderstanding of God. But his criticism is motivated by his concern for them. It would not have been love to write them out of his life.

A Caring God

The message of Jesus, in word or deed, was *diakonia*, service. He had come as the caring physician, the friend of the outcast. His warm concern for the "poor," the little ones, brought him into conflict with those whose understanding of God was so different from his. Because he would not brand anyone an outcast, because he put ethics in place of ritual preoccupation, because he set people above observance, he was classed as a breaker of the law, as one who did not do the will of God. He remained faithful to the God he knew and he responded to the will of his loving Father — though that faithfulness took him to the cross. His death set humankind free because his life was laid down in defence of the value and dignity of the human person. In his life, sealed by the integrity of his death, Jesus gave expression to God's respect for humankind.

For this Jesus had been sent: to display the limitless love of the Father for humankind. He manifested that Father's love through his own loving concern for and service of all. Nothing would turn him from that way of love. He would lay down his life in the task — even when it meant that life being crushed from him by those who could not or would not understand his service of love. But the Father understood that in this unswerving faithfulness to love lay the destruction of evil. This, too, in what Jesus meant when he spoke in the supper room of "my body which is given for you" (Lk 22:19). Or when, in John, he spoke of that love than which none is greater, "that a man lay down his life for his friends" (Jn 12:13).

The Son knew the Father and came to do his will. His life was not laid down in answer to a divine need. It was laid down in answer to divine love. Father and Son were prepared to go to any length to save man from himself. Here I might observe that I have long rejected the Anselmian theory of satisfaction in any shape or form.[1] It seems incredible that for nearly a thousand years it has prevailed — in spite of the fact that it is a travesty of the gospel and draws a caricature of God. It is tragic that this theological theory has had such a long and widespread effect on christian piety. The truth is that Jesus will save humankind though it cost him his life. And it did. And there, I believe, we find the ultimate meaning of the cry: "My God, my God, why have you abandoned me?" (Mk 15:34). Jesus is letting

[1]See p. 129.

God be God. For it is in and through that emptiness — that openness — of the Son that the Father has given us everything, that he has made us his daughters and his sons.

Jesus did not come preaching a "new religion." He had no intention of starting something new. He came to renew Israel. His call was for *metanoia,* a radical change of heart. A surely authentic word of Jesus (because it must have been embarrassing for a church that had turned to the Gentiles) is the declaration: "I was sent only to the lost sheep of the house of Israel" (Mt 15:24; cp 10:6). He had come to summon Israel to become what God wanted his people to be. He had caught up the clarion call of the Baptist and made it his own. Inherent in Jesus' vision, however, was a dimension that, eventually, would no longer fit the old wineskin.

Jesus began his mission with optimism. He did not start off with a grim vision of a violent death at the end of the road. But as his mission progressed, he had to come to terms with the reaction and opposition that forced him to reckon with, first, the possibility and, then, the probability, of violent death. It is likely that the temptation stories, put at the start of the ministry by Matthew and Luke, really concern decisions made at a later stage. Certainly, Gethsemane and the anguished cry from the cross witness to the agony of decision and the depressing prospect of failure.

Forgiveness

Many Christians (especially Catholics) would be more disturbed than the elder son if they permitted themselves to dwell on the subversive drift of the Prodigal Son (Lk 15:11-

32). It may be that Luke had a hand in the final shape of the story; the substance of it has to come from Jesus himself. And the Lucan setting would fix it, readily, in the ministry of Jesus: "The Pharisees and scribes murmured, saying, 'This man receives sinners and eats with them'" (Lk 15:2). Jesus' parable is a defence of his own conduct, his concern for the "little ones" whom the Pharisees had written off as outcasts. Defence, yes — but profoundly challenging.

Jesus' Jewish hearers would have grasped the pathos of the young man's plight: a Jew herding pigs! He had hit rockbottom. What they would have found disconcerting was the incredible conduct of the father. To receive back without word of reproof and without any condition at all one who had shown himself so weak, was unbelievably foolish. They would have identified, readily, with the hardnosed other son. The fact that the story itself manifestly extols the conduct of the father would have given pause. What is it all about?

Jesus would suggest that the weakness and the strength of the younger son is vulnerability. He is vulnerable both to his fairweather friends and to the love of his father. In contrast, the rectitude of the elder son is effective armour against the plea of vulnerability and the foolishness of love. He had never really known his father and he now rejects his brother who had besmirched the family name. Had he not a point? To receive back, without sanctions, one who had already proved fickle, was rash in the extreme. It was crass favouritism — this cossetting of a profligate and neglect of one who had always served and obeyed.

This is a disturbing story, on many counts — a disturbing story for us Christians of today. Luke had already taken it out of the ministry of Jesus and addressed it directly to the "pharisees" of his own community. And surely we must look to ourselves, to our possible resentment at God's graciousness to sinners. We can find comfort in the warm treatment of the younger son. Always there is the father. He is the real challenge. For this story of the father and his two sons is allegory; the characters are God, the sinner and the righteous. The gracious, forgiving Father holds the stage.

The father is God eagerly looking for the first steps of homecoming. After that initial turning on the part of the sinner, the action is all his. The son had gone away as son and had come back a pitiful tramp. He was reinstated without any condition at all; he is son as though he had never left. There is no confession before forgiveness because there is no place for it in this Father's forgiveness. The declaration of unworthiness comes as a response to forgiveness. It is not easy to discover in Jesus' picture of God's loving forgiveness any basis for that "temporal debt due to sin" that was so much part of a former catechesis. We grudge God the graciousness of his forgiveness.

What does this powerful story say to me? It speaks, eloquently, of a loving God's concern for humankind, in particular of his "favoritism" towards the outcast. It sets a question mark against the theology of forgiveness reflected in much of our penitential practice. God's forgiveness is just too good to be true. Above all, there is the uncomfortable truth that one really gets to know this Father only by acknowledging the brother and sister as brother and sister —a lesson learned by the author of 1 John: "The person who does not love his brother whom he has seen, cannot love God whom he has not seen" (4:20). It is dangerous to listen to this kind of story.

Her Great Love

There remains the central reality of forgiveness. Too often God's deed is set in a grim context of reparation that strips it of its graciousness. What ought to follow on forgiveness is loving response. This lesson is touchingly taught by Luke: his story of "a woman of the city who was a sinner" (Lk 7:36-50). She was a woman who had previously encountered Jesus and had received his forgiveness. She came, now, to make a brave and extravagant gesture. She crashed a stag-party and anointed and kissed the feet of a reclining Jesus — to the evident scandal of his pharisee host. Jesus accepted her presence and ministering with gentle courtesy. And his verdict was clear and to the point: "her great love proves that her sins have been forgiven" (7:47). One is not casual in the face of forgiveness. But response to it is not by way of "making up" to an offended deity.

Acknowledgment of forgiveness received can be expressed in other ways than the anointing of the feet of Jesus. The best way of all is by extension of forgiveness to others. In Matthew's parable of the Unmerciful Servant we meet again the sinner and his God (Mt 18:23-35). An impossible debt is casually written off in response to the sinner's plea. And the man is not even sacked. Like the younger son of Luke's parable he is restored without any strings. Faced with a cry of desperation, the forgiving God was moved with pity (v. 27). But when the recipient of such forgiveness cannot find it in his heart to be merciful, the Master is angry (v.3). Response to God's gracious forgiveness cannot be payment of a debt that is already fully remitted. It is, instead, warm thanksgiving for the blessing of such forgiving love. And the

Matthean story underlines again that sin, as God regards it, is man's inhumanity to man — whatever shape that may take. Our abuse of others (and of ourselves) is an affront to the loving Father who counts us as his children. This, Jesus so clearly understood because he knew his Father.

It Shall Not Be So

Jesus did not set out to challenge head-on the structures of oppression; or, at least, he did not do so openly in the political and social fields. It was different in the sphere of religion. There the clash was unavoidable.[2] In other areas his approach and his message, while not adding up to a direct attack on social attitudes and practices, was effectively subversive of them. Indeed, one might go further and maintain that while his attack on "unclean spirits" was, in fact, an attack on disease, his war against "Satan" was war against oppressive power structures and dehumanizing power systems. Jesus always aimed at the root causes. It is not surprising, then, that there is no evidence of his ever taking a stand against Roman oppression. For that matter, when challenged, he declared: "Render to Caesar what is Caesar's and to God what is God's" (Mk 12:17). His whole teaching made clear his assumption that Caesar's claim would be just: he does not give Caesar a blank check. And never would he envisage violence as a way to political and social change. His demand, "Love your enemy," is a radical disavowal of violence. It is a challenge which carries within it the seed of the destruction of violence.

[2]See p. 64.

A Turn from Patriarchy

The Jewish social world of Jesus' day was firmly patriarchal. It was a model that he looked at, and rejected. That rejection was something traditional exegesis had not discerned; today we view the texts with clearer perception.[3] There was no place for patriarchal structure in Jesus' model of community. A consistent picture emerges when we follow up the texts:

> If any one would be first, he must be last of all and servant of all. And he took a child, and put him in the midst of them and took him in his arms (Mk 9:35-36). Let the children come to me, do not hinder them; for to such belongs the kingdom of God. Truly, I say to you, whoever does not receive the kingdom of God like a child shall not enter it. And he took them in his arms and blessed them, laying his hands upon them (10: 14-16). You know that those who are supposed to rule over the Gentiles lord it over them. But is shall not be so among you; but whoever would be great among you would be your servant, and whoever would be first among you must be slave of all. For the son of man also came not to be served but to serve, and to give his life as a ransom for many. (10:42-45)

The first thing to note is that child/slave has become the model for discipleship. The status of a slave is self-evident. And, in a patriarchal household, the status of a child was no better than that of a slave — witness the admonitions in the wisdom literature on the discipling of sons (e.g. Prov 23:13-14; Sirach 30:1-13). The child/slave model is a radical challenge to patriarchal structure; it is a demand for the relinquishing of all claims of power and domination over others. In speaking of "servant" and "slave" Jesus is

[3]See p. 54.

addressing a society in which masters and slaves exist and, in the name of the rule of God, he is challenging that structure. He calls on masters to relinquish dominion, to "serve" — in other words, to acknowledge, wholly, the dignity of those who are their "servants." This challenge is subversive of all structures based on domination.

Jesus' call has special relevance within his own movement and for his followers. Leadership in his movement must wear the unmistakable livery of *diakonia*, of service. Any suggestion of dominance, any vestige of oppression, must stand as a denial of him and all he represents. In this regard what came to be his church has much to learn and much more to unlearn.

In the context of Mark 10:35-37 — the demand of the sons of Zebedee for first places in the kingdom — Jesus solemnly asserts that in the community of his disciples there is no place for ambition. As his movement grew into a church, the need for authority inevitably arose, and the exercise of authority within the church has been a problem, from the start. The church is a human society: there is need for authority, there must be leaders. But those who lead will serve their brothers and sisters; the spirit of authority is *diakonia*. Surely, Jesus has intended the paradox and asks for it to be taken seriously. There is the shining light of his own example: he served God's purpose, the salvation of men and women, by laying down his life in the service of humankind. There really can be no justification at all for the style and trappings and exercise of authority inspired by the powers and princes of this world. Centuries of tradition should not weigh against the stark words of the Lord. *It shall not be so among you* — we have no right to urge the weight of history against a demand as clear as that. Sooner or later we must find the courage to admit that, not only in word but in deed, we have not hearkened to this word of the Lord.

Service in Love

"But it shall not be so among you." One has often thought that these words are, in their way, the saddest in the gospels. They are so unambiguous; they not only express what Jesus said more than once but reflect his manner of life. And yet ... the form and exercise of authority in the church has been, almost from the start, and continues to be, the antithesis of Jesus' demand. He tells us that the community of his disciples is not to take the form of a power-structure. He asks that those in authority in his community be the servants of those whom they lead. No, not only the "servant," Jesus boldly declares, but *the slave of all*. The great Paul was unashamed not only to call himself but to make himself "a slave of all" (1 Cor 9:19; cf. 2 Cor 4:5). Thus he could, with so much greater authority, urge his disciples to be servants of one another in the service of love (Gal 5:13). This service ennobles because it is a service of disinterested love and is consistent with true freedom. For it is the service of setting others free to achieve their full potential in Christ. Those words of Jesus are crystal clear: unlike worldly rulers, concerned with power and glory, his disciples are to serve without pomp and display. His demand is not covered by such a title as *servus servorum Dei*. There must be some substance behind the title — and so on down the line.

The ground of the paradoxical behaviour required of

disciples is the example of Jesus himself: "For the Son of man also came not to be served but to serve and to give his life as a ransom for many" (Mk 10:45). His service of men and women reached to the laying down of life itself. In its Marcan form the saying is related to Isaiah 53:10-11 and the "ransom" (*lytron*) is to be understood in the sense of the Hebrew *asham* of Isaiah 53:10, an "offering for sin," an expiation. By laying down his life for a humankind enslaved to sin, Jesus fulfils the saying about the servant. This interpretation of the death of Jesus shows christian theology at work. It is a true interpretation not alone of his death but of his life. Jesus laid down his life not only on the cross but in his life-style of service.

Another revealing text is Matthew 23:8-11. Obviously, Matthew is exercised by developments in his community, with leaders arrogating titles to themselves. Leaders were no longer content with being servants of the community —they wanted to be "real" leaders. The titles claimed were those of "rabbi," "father" and "teacher."

> But you are not to be called rabbi, for you have one teacher and you are all brethren. And call no one your father on earth, for you have one Father, who is in heaven. Neither be called masters, for you have one master, the Christ. (Mt 23:8-10)

Even if the passage, as it stands, does not go back to Jesus, it is an accurate reflection of his attitude and demands. The title Rabbi — literally, "my great one" — would sit incongruously on one who is "slave" of the community. Nor is any to be addressed as "teacher," "master" — practically the same as "rabbi." Since God alone is Father no one in the community is "father." Clearly, for Matthew, desire for that

title is affectation, a questing for prestige. Further, it marks a
retrograde step: it asserts the standards of patriarchal culture.
Jesus had looked for a discipleship of equals.[4] We shall see in
the following chapter how the example of the teaching and
praxis of Jesus, if given a chance, could have radically affected
the status of women in the community of his disciples.

[4] "If Matthew's church were at Antioch in Syria the place where the monar-
chical episcopate arose around the time of Ignatius of Antioch, one can conclude
that Matthew's indignant protests against titles were canonized but not heard.
The Catholic Church in particular must reflect on whether these inspired words
call it to forsake the ecclesiastical titles which have proliferated in its midst,
especially since one of its most common titles, 'Father,' is specifically forbidden to
religious leaders." John Meier, *Matthew* (Wilmington, DE: M. Glazier, 1980,
256).

4

JESUS AND WOMEN

The Jewish society of Jesus' day was solidly patriarchal. Women had few legal rights and were, in theory and in practice, second-class citizens. So, for instance, divorce, as a male prerogative, militated severely against them. Together with children they were dispensed from the daily prayer obligation of the adult male Jew, attended the synagogue in silent isolation, and were debarred from all levels of priestly service. It does not follow that they were hopelessly passive. Frequent references in Proverbs and Sirach to the "nagging wife" is a wry acknowledgment of the practical self-assertiveness of women who, socially and legally, were ostensibly powerless. But none of that disguises the simple fact that women were trapped in a patriarchal world. If Jesus had come to proclaim God's opposition to all oppression of people he could not have been aloof to the oppression of women. And he was not.

At this point we need to advert to the androcentric ("male-centered") character of the New Testament. And we need to take into account that the New Testament canon, which took shape under pressure of various factors, is "a theological document of the 'historical winners'."[1] One important factor in the shaping of the canon was the bitter struggle in the second and third centuries concerning the role of women in the church. In the event, victory went to the forces opposed to the leadership claims and practice of women. It was inevitable that writings with an androcentric bias would prevail.

If one is not aware of this situation, then one will readily assume that the discreet presence of women in the pages of the New Testament means that the passive role which was to be theirs in later centuries was a fact of life from the start. Indeed, the situation is worse than it might seem at first sight because, for most of the time, women figure at all only when they are exceptional or (and the fact speaks for itself) when women's behavior presents a problem. Consequently, the sparsity of reference to women in the New Testament writings is no indication of a corresponding minimal role for them. Especially in the case of Jesus and Paul one may discern, through the gospel text and the Pauline letters, a remarkable prominence of women in the Jesus movement and in the early christian movement. It is not enough, then, to look only to passages where women are mentioned. One must be alert to the fact that women are often present where there is no specific reference to them. We have been challenged to look at the New Testament in a fresh light. For

---

[1] Elizabeth Schüssler Fiorenza, *In Memory of Her,* A Feminist Theological Reconstruction of Christian Origins (New York: Crossroad, 1983, xv).

any who are prepared to acknowledge the scholarly integrity of the challenge, the New Testament can never look quite the same again.

The Good News

We have seen that "preaching good news to the poor" could and did characterize the whole of Jesus' ministry, provided one grants to the term "poor" its widest range of meaning. The "poor" are the broken-hearted, the captives, those who are faint of spirit; the "poor" are the oppressed, the marginalized. It surely must be that a large, if not the greater number, of the "poor" were women. Yet, how rarely does that simple fact emerge in exegesis! If his mission were "good news to the poor," then Jesus' contact with women, still visible in the gospel traditions, must have been vastly more prevalent than our sources would seem to allow. "The poor *have* the good news preached to them" — Jesus is not promising future recompense, nor any reversal of roles. He is asserting the rights of the poor and invoking God's justice which is vindication of the poor. And the poor include women, not only inevitably so in the nature of things but also in view of the "widow and orphan," the archetypical poor of biblical tradition. It surely must be perfectly obvious that "poor" is an inclusive term.

But so, too, is the term "disciple"! This is evident in Mark. The women ("Mary Magdalene, and Mary the mother of James the younger and of Joses, and Salome") who, standing at a distance, witnessed the crucifixion of Jesus, are described as those who "followed him" — a technical term for discipleship. For that matter, the "many other women" mentioned in the same context are also disciples (Mk 15:40-41). It is, of course, true that Luke speaks of these Galilean women only as "providing for them (Jesus and the Twelve) out of their means" (Lk 8:3). While that material provision may well have been welcome, failure to designate these women as disciples is tendentious. After all, Luke is a representative of "early Catholicism," one of whose characteristics is an erosion of women's leadership roles in the communities. The fact remains that much androcentric language really carries a generic sense. It should be helpful now to look at gospel passages where women do explicitly figure. From these we may better appreciate the need to be more circumspect in our reading of the whole text.

Discipleship of Equals

It is clear that the women of Jesus' Jewish society suffered under patriarchal structures. Not in formal, but in effective, contrast Jesus established his discipleship of equals. Because we had simply gone along with a traditional androcentric approach to the gospel text, we had missed the significance of certain passages — such as Mark 10:29-30. There Jesus speaks of renunciation and gift: "Truly, I say to you, there is no one who has left house or brothers or sisters or mother or father or children or lands, for my sake and for the gospel, who will not receive a hundredfold now in this time, houses and brothers and sisters and mothers and children and lands, with persecutions, and in the age to come eternal life." "Fathers" are significantly absent from the second list. There is no place for patriarchal structures in Jesus' community. The sword text of Matthew 10:34-36 ("I have not come to bring peace, but a sword. For I have come to set a man against his father, and a daughter against her mother . . .") points in the same direction. "The sword brought by Jesus cuts the bond uniting the generations, thus effectively destroying the patriarchal family."[2] And, as for the place of women in his movement, there is the telling passage of Mark 3:31-35. While Jesus' "mother and his brothers" (vv 31,32) had sent to summon him, Jesus' reply was to designate those who "do the will of God" — surely, in the context, true disciples —as "my brother, and *sister and mother*" (v. 35).

I have done enough, I believe, to show that women are by no means absent from what is, in the main, an androcentric text. Indeed, there is some concern to present them in a favorable color. One might even say that the real trouble has not been the text itself but a consistently androcentric reading of the text over nineteen centuries. Only in our day do we have exegetes who are prepared to ask other questions of the text. And one of these questions concerns the presence and place of women in the Jesus movement. The answer is startling. The answer challenges nineteen centuries of christian attitudes and practice.

Mark has a number of significant encounters of Jesus with women. All of them are overlaid with Marcan theology. Nevertheless, in some of them at least, we can discern clear evidence, not only of Jesus' sensitive attitude to women but, too, of their trusting rapport with him. There is the woman with the haemorrhage (Mk 5:25-34). According to the pre-

[2]Jerome Murphy-O'Connor, "A Feminist Re-reads the New Testament," *Doctrine and Life* 34 (1984), 401.

scriptions of Leviticus 15:19-28 such a one was ritually unclean. She had no business being in a crowd and acted quite wrongly in touching Jesus' garment and making him also ritually unclean. But she obviously knew her man and was not disappointed. The story shows Jesus deliberately ignoring restrictive purity obligations, shows him intent only on liberation from physical and social suffering. Instead of reprimanding her for her "reprehensible" conduct, he acknowledges her as "daughter" and heals her.

The Quickwitted Woman (Mk 7:24-30)

Another woman who met Jesus was "a Greek, a Syrophoenician by birth" — in other words, a Gentile by birth and religion. Her request for the healing of her daughter was refused because, as Jesus tells her, the rules did not allow it. His mission was to the chosen people: His "bread" was not for "dogs" — a contemptuous Jewish label for Gentiles. She will not be put off: all very well indeed — but even the dogs get crumbs! And Jesus responded to the challenge. "To our staid mentality it seems inappropriate, even shocking that Jesus would change his mind about the scope of his mission because a woman, and a pagan at that, challenged him to think again. Should we not instead, like Jesus, allow ourselves to think again and in our Church today, with the same persistent trust in Jesus, speak out the challenging of our deep aspirations — not out of aggressiveness and frustration but from genuine conviction."[3]

[3]Eleanor Dorgan, "The Women in Mark's Gospel," *Scripture in Church* No. 52 (1983), 499.

The Anointing (14:3-9)

Mark has located his story of the anointing of Jesus at Bethany (14:3) in the house of "Simon the leper," doubtless one known in the circle where the story originated. The woman is not named: interest falls on the saying (vv 7-9). She is obviously a disciple — how else could one account for her gesture? By her anointing of Jesus' head the woman is symbolically proclaiming him as the Messiah, the Anointed of God (cf 2 Kgs 9:1-13; 1 Kgs 1:38-40). She, however vaguely, has recognized him as Israel's Messiah. Jesus graciously accepts anointing — but relates it to his death. The woman has made a lovely gesture, more meaningful than she knew; she, the woman-disciple, shows an understanding that the men-disciples lack (Mt 26:8). Her gracious deed will win her immortality: "Truly, I say to you, where ever the gospel is preached in the whole world, what she has done will be told in memory of her" (14:9). Here, surely, one cannot blame the gospel text: the deed of this woman is firmly highlighted. But what has happened to the story in christian tradition? Has that "beautiful thing" become a familiar part of the gospel knowledge of Christians? "Wherever the gospel is proclaimed and the eucharist celebrated another story is told: the story of the apostle who betrayed Jesus. The name of the betrayer is remembered, but the name of the faithful disciple is forgotten because she was a woman."[4] Has anyone got a better explanation?

---

[4] E. Schüssler Fiorenza, *op. cit.*, xiii. The Judas story (14:1-2, 10-11) frames the anointing.

The Pardoned Sinner (Lk 7:36-50)

While the anointing of Jesus related in Mark 14:39 and John 12:1-8 are differing versions of the same incident, the anointing in Luke 7:36-50 points to another episode. Of course, in the telling, details have floated back and forth across the stories. Luke's woman is a "sinner" (vv 37,39), and we should rest content with the vagueness of the designation. What we must presume is that she and Jesus had met and that she had received, through him, the gracious forgiveness of the Father. That is surely the drift of the little parable (vv 41-43) and is explicit in the declaration of Jesus: "her great love proves that her many sins have been forgiven" (v. 47). She had come — a woman and a "sinner" to boot —and crashed a stag-party. She most certainly did not belong (v. 39). Hers was a brave and extravagant gesture of thanksgiving. This woman, too, had done a "beautiful thing" to Jesus and he received her ministration with typical graciousness. Who can doubt that this woman had become a disciple?

The Faithful Women

The men disciples of Jesus had abandoned him and fled for their lives (Mk 14:50). The women disciples did not lose heart: they followed him as far as women might, looking on the crucifixion-scene "from afar" (15:40). Mark names three of the group — the impression is of a relatively large group. All of these women are firmly cast as disciples. They were Galileans who had "followed" Jesus and had "come up with him" to Jerusalem — again, discipleship. It is because they had continued to follow him, if even "from afar," that the final message is entrusted to them. They alone, of all others, had followed to the cross. The chosen men disciples had abandoned Jesus. These women disciples have stood steadfast and have not been ashamed of Jesus (8:38).

But have not the women, too, failed at the end? They were given a message: "Go, tell his disciples and Peter that he is going before you to Galilee" (16:7). But what kind of messengers did they turn out to be? — "they said nothing to anyone, for they were afraid" (v. 8). Relevant here is 10:32. There Jesus is presented as going up to Jerusalem, striding ahead of his disciples who were "filled with awe ... and were afraid." But their fear did not paralyse them from following Jesus.[5] So with the women who had come to the tomb to honor one who was dead. They find themselves faced with the awesome truth of the Living One. They are in the grip of trembling and "ecstasy." "They therefore leave in 'fear,' gripped by the same wondrous awe that had stunned biblical witnesses from Moses to Paul. The fearful and resplendent presence of the living God was now seen as never before in the crucified Messiah's victory over death."[6] The women had not failed: Mark's gospel is the proof of it! Obviously, Peter and the other men and women disciples *had* been told. And is it not thought-provoking that so much scholarly concern has focused on the "problem" of the "failure" of the women. Much less interest, let it be said, has

[5]Marla J. Selvidge, "'And Those Who Followed Feared' (Mk 10:32)," *Catholic Biblical Quarterly* 45 (1983), 400.

[6]Donald Senior, *The Passion of Jesus in the Gospel of Mark* (Wilmington, DE: M. Glazier, 1984, 137).

attached to the disturbing fact that it was women who were "apostles to the apostles."

Mary Magdalene

The fourth evangelist has heightened the effect by concentrating the woman-witness in the dramatic figure of Mary Magdalene. And just here, it seems to me, one can, in conclusion, effectively highlight, in terms of the fate of Mary, the fate of women throughout christian tradition. Tradition has been cruel to Mary Magdalene. Indeed, she could well qualify as the most sinned against victim of sexist prejudice. Her characterization as a reformed prostitute has gone almost unchallenged. The fact is: there is not a single shred of evidence to sustain that portrait of her. She has had the ill fortune to emerge for the first time in Luke's gospel immediately after his story of "the sinner" (Lk 7:36-50). Whether or not that "sinner" was a prostitute (not at all clear) has nothing to do with the subsequent reference to "Mary, called Magdalene, from whom seven demons had gone out" (8:2). Traditionally, the "seven demons" have been interpreted as demons of sexual immorality and Mary has been identified with the anonymous woman of chapter 7 (who was regarded as a prostitute). The only logic here is the sick logic of misogyny. From parallel texts it is clear that possession by "seven demons" means that Mary was a mentally ill woman, healed by Jesus. To class her as "sinner" is calumny.

In simple justice, the christian rehabilitation of Mary Magdalene is long overdue. One is not suggesting that a onetime sinner might not become a follower of Jesus and a saint. But there is no excuse for classifying Mary Magdalene as a reformed prostitute. Perhaps the whole of feminist unhappiness with the church is just there. The thoroughly positive presentation of Mary Magdalene in the synoptic — and more so in the Johannine — traditions has been adroitly manipulated. The threatening Mary has been cut down to size: she is the proverbial prostitute with the heart of gold.

Fidelity

By dwelling on the faithful women and the seeming digression on Mary Magdalene, I appear to have departed from my brief: Jesus and women. Not so. Whatever later tradition may have made of it, there remains the sturdy fidelity of these women — with Mary as staunchest among them. That fidelity is their response to something that touched them deeply. They, to an extent that men disciples in that patriarchal society could not feel, experienced the magic of being accepted as and for their womanly selves. For the first time they really knew equality. In encounter with Jesus they *experienced* the truth of what Paul was to proclaim: ". . . no male and female, for you are all one in Christ" (Gal 3:28).

How, then, after two millennia of Christianity is it that christian women have to *fight* for equality? What has gone wrong? A new reading of the gospels may, if we have the will, enable us to see what we have failed to see. A new openness to the Man Christ Jesus may bring us to realize that his sisters are just as fully his disciples as are his brothers. The questions are: Does our church want to see? And, were it to see, would it have the will to act?

5

JESUS AND RELIGION

The synoptists proclaim that "the kingdom of God" was Jesus' central message. What Jesus meant by "kingdom of God" — better "rule of God" — was a situation in which God acts as king and lord, a situation in which his Godhead is manifest in the world of humankind. God is not a king who lords it over his subjects. Throughout the Bible the coming of the kingdom is the coming of God as salvation for human beings.

What Jesus meant by God's "lordship" is finely caught by the author of the letter to Titus: "When the goodness and loving kindness of God our Savior appeared, he saved us, not because of deeds done by us in righteousness, but in virtue of his own mercy" (Titus 3:4-5). The God of Jesus is a God who has supreme concern for people. His lordship points to an ideal, God-willed relationship between God and human-kind, reflected in a new relationship between human beings, a relationship lived within a peaceful, reconciling society:

"How those Christians love one another!" Jesus lived and died for the establishment of that rule. He ached for men and women to discover the love of God for humankind and give substance to the wonder of the discovery in loving concern for one another.

In preaching the rule of God, Jesus was defining God; he was proclaiming a God bent on the salvation of humankind. That is why he proclaimed good news to the poor — the needy of every sort, the outcast. That is why he was friend of sinners — why he had tablefellowship with sinners. It was precisely because, in deed and word, he tirelessly preached a God of mercy that he ended up on a cross. That God was unacceptable to the religious people of his day.

The Authority of Jesus

It is clear from the gospels that Jesus had *exousia* — authority — from God. It is equally clear that this power of his did not have any shade of domination. Mark does indeed show Jesus having facile authority over evil spirits — the exorcisms, and over nature — the stilling of the tempest. But Jesus' authority does not extend itself to lording it over *people*. For that matter, in relation to people, he is largely helpless. The hallmark of the use of his authority in relation to people is consistently and emphatically that of *diakonia*, "service." But if Jesus does serve others, it is always from a position of strength. He will not do what others want him to do unless it be consonant with God's will. He will lead, but he will not control. He healed, both physically and spiritually, looking for nothing else than openness to his healing touch. He was friend of sinners — and we must not allow ourselves sub-consciously to think that they were repentant sinners before he was their friend. No, he befriended them in their brokenness.

Jesus served his disciples. Though their misunderstanding is a distinctive Marcan theme, their failure, candidly admitted by all three synoptists, is unquestionably historical. He would not manipulate them; he respected their freedom. He would not force their loyalty. What won them, ultimately, was the startling experience that, when they encountered their Master beyond death, they heard no word of blame. There was nothing but love and the most exquisite forgiveness. "Go and tell my brothers . . ."

Jesus certainly confronted the authorities, but without seeking to impose his authority on them. He was content to hold the mirror up to them, urging them to see in their attitude and conduct a betrayal of God's rule. But that was the measure of it. Response was their responsibility.

Jesus sought no advantage from his authority. He laid claim to no titles — it was up to others to identify him. He referred to himself simply as "son of man." Of course, in the gospels "Son of Man" is a christological title. It seems to me though, as I have observed earlier, that it is becoming clearer that Jesus' use of the title had no theological bias. Quite the contrary. He was the "one" who had nowhere to lay his head, the "man" who made no personal claims, the "man" who depended wholly on God for his being and his authority.

Though Jesus had never lorded it over people, he had never shrunk from challenging oppressive attitudes and practices. In doing so he became the man who relieved suffering. But at the end he was the vulnerable one who became a victim of suffering. He was, after all, the one who had come "to serve, and to give his life as a ransom for many" (10:45). In short, Jesus, in his authority as in all else, mirrored God. For God, the God of infinite power, is never a God of force. The Son never did, nor ever would, resort to force.[1]

We do not hear of Jesus having much truck with priests. This may be because he did not spend much time in Jerusalem — though here the Johannine tradition should be reckoned with. Rather, it seems to be that though he could engage readily enough with Pharisees he did not have an easy rapport with the priestly class. They would have looked on him with disdain. But there is more to it. "Clericalism" was repugnant to Jesus. His view of authority in the kingdom was consciously paradoxical: authority was *diakonia*, service. Matthew, faced with incipient clericalism in his own community, has accurately spelled out the implication of Jesus' concept of religious authority: "You are not to be called rabbi ... and call no one your father on earth ... neither be called masters" (Mt 23:8-10). When authority is characterized as "service" then human standards are stood on their head. How radical that demand is may be seen from the problem that authority always has been and continues to be within the christian churches. It is fatally easy to take on, with authority, the worldly modes and trappings of it. "It shall not be so among you" (Mk 10:42-45, parr.) Jesus was not understood in his own day. Nor has he really been understood ever since. Least of all, perhaps, by professional churchmen.

[1]David Rhoads and Donald Michie, *Mark as Story* (Philadelphia: Fortress Press, 1982, 103-116).

He Declared All Foods Clean

A precise incident lies behind the dispute of Jesus with the Pharisees and scribes related in Mark 7:1-23 — they had observed that the disciples of Jesus did not perform the ritual washing of hands before meals. In their eyes that constituted a transgression of the "tradition of the elders," the *halakah*, the oral law. Jesus responds to the criticism. He does not confine himself to the particular point of ritual purification but turns the debate on to a wider issue. He cites Isaiah 29:13 against the Pharisees, drawing a parallel between the "precepts of men" of which Isaiah speaks, and the "tradition of men" on which the Pharisees count. Implicitly, he accuses them of putting their traditions on the same level, as, or, in practical terms, even above, the Law of God. Jesus rejected the *halakah* because it was a merely human system and because it could conflict with the law of God. This human law had put casuistry above love.

The principle of clean and unclean was at the root of Jewish concern over ritual purification. A saying of Jesus —"There is nothing outside a man which by going into him can defile him; but the things which come out of a man are what defile him" (Mk 7:15) — points out that sin, which alone defiles a man, comes from within oneself; it is more important to be concerned about evil thoughts and sinful deeds than about ceremonial purity. The broad implication of the saying, which set aside the law of cultic purity, was recognized in a gentile-christian setting (vv. 18-23). It is made clear to these Christians that being followers of Christ does not require the observance of Jewish practices. The door is truly open to all.

The deepest reason why the Marcan Jesus rejected the "tradition of the elders" and annulled the concept of cultic impurity is because another and more efficacious economy had come into being. The argument of Mark 7:14-23 is remarkably like that of Hebrews 9-10. Like the author of the epistle, Jesus shows that legal discrimination between clean and unclean is incapable of really purifying the human heart; for it cannot be more than a provisional expedient. And if Jesus can *now* pronounce the disposition obsolete it is for one reason: because the definitive order has brought the provisional order to an end. This is not formulated but it is presupposed, and Mark suggests this meaning by means of the reproach of 7:18 — "Do you not see that whatever goes into a man from outside cannot defile him." Jesus' abolition of the Jewish cultic tradition of clean and unclean manifests to whomever can understand that a new order has emerged (cf 2:21-22).

The sweeping range of Mark 7:15 becomes apparent when one compares it with Matthew 15:11 — "Not what goes into the mouth defiles a man, but what comes out of the mouth, this defiles a man," and the apocryphal *Gospel of Thomas* — "For what enters into your mouth will not defile you." Both texts are obviously concerned with sins of the tongue; Mark's version is a principle of universal import: "there is nothing outside a man . . . the things which come out of a man . . ." Structured as antithetical parallelism, this saying is radical and strikes at the very distinction of clean and unclean, of sacred and secular. Not surprisingly, it has no parallel in Judaism for it denies a basic principle of Jewish religion and sets aside a large area of Mosaic Torah. It is a flat denial that any external things or circumstances can separate a man from God (cf Rom 8:38-39). We can be separated from God only by our own attitude and behavior.

The Sabbath Was Made for Man

The wisdom saying of Mark 2:27 — "The sabbath was made for man, not man for the sabbath" — has a close enough rabbinical parallel: "The sabbath is delivered unto you; you are not delivered to the sabbath."[2] In both cases the meaning of the saying is that God ordained the sabbath for man's sake; it is a reaction against a false evaluation of the sabbath whereby man becomes a slave to sabbath observance. In a rabbinical setting the declaration would have to stand agains the backdrop of reverence for Torah. For Jesus, "sabbath" is a symbol for religion. What he means is: "Religion was made for man, not man for religion." He, better than any other, was conscious of the oppressive force of religion. He fell victim to organized religion. Conflict between Jesus and the religious authorities of Judaism is well documented. It is an aspect of the ministry that, if anything, grew in the telling — as in Matthew 13. Though these "Woes" represent a beleaguered Jewish-Christian community hitting back at Jewish opposition, their scathing castigation of legalism has support in the attitude and life-style of Jesus. We shall see that Paul — the former Pharisee — had indeed grasped the message of Jesus.

[2]*Mekilta* on Ex 31:14.

You Did It to Me

Jesus had come to bear witness to the God he knew as Father. How are we to treat one who, in response to the Father's love of humankind, has spent himself to his dying breath? And what kind of God do we see revealed in him?

> We have seen what Jesus was like. If we now wish to treat him as our God, we would have to conclude that our God does not want to be served by us, he wants to serve us; he does not want to be given the highest possible rank and status in our society; he does not want to be feared and obeyed, he wants to be recognized in the suffering of the poor and the weak; he is not supremely indifferent and detached, he is irrevocably committed to the liberation of mankind, for he has chosen to identify himself with all men in a spirit of solidarity and compassion. If this is not a true picture of God, then Jesus is not divine. If this is a true picture of God, then God is more truly human, more thoroughly humane than any human being. He is what Schillebeeckx has called a *Deus humanissimus,* a supremely human God.[3]

Somewhat by way of confirmation we may find, with special clarity, Jesus' understanding of the Father where we might not expect to find it: in Matthew's great scene of the Last Judgment (Mt 25:31-46). Rightly to appreciate this passage one must understand that it is retrospective. Matthew has in mind how Jesus comported himself — how he related to people. What Jesus did and said becomes the standard of judgment. He had come, a man, into our human

[3]Albert Nolan, *Jesus Before Christianity* (New York: Orbis Books, 1978, 137-138).

history, to tell us of the Godness of God. Jesus taught and lived that the reality of God is revealed in the realization of more humanity between fellow human beings — giving drink to the thirsty, feeding the hungry, welcoming the stranger. Matthew's story of judgment is focussed on purely human concerns. But these are God's concern: "Come, you blessed of my Father." The emphasis is on the needy person, the one in distress. What is at stake in this last judgment is our attitude towards the little ones, the humble and the needy. The criterion is not the standard of religion or cult; it is, starkly: has one helped those in need.

The scene is vivid. Mixed flocks of (white) sheep and (black) goats were a common sight in Palestine. Here sheep and goats separate for final blessing or curse. The King of the heavenly kingdom sits in judgment on his people. The good works of vv. 34-36 are the traditional "corporal works of mercy" and the elect have performed these works. Their surprise, their amazement, is in being told by the king that they had done them "to me." Astounded, they ask: "When? ... when? ... when? ..." The answer is Jesus' solemn attestation of his total identification with the poor and out-cast and oppressed. It might seem, at first sight, that this Matthean scene has nothing specifically Christian about it. But when we realize that nothing less than the comportment of Jesus himself is the yardstick of judgment, we can see how thoroughly Christian it is. And this is so even though it embraces "all the nations" — all people without distinction (25:32).

The truth is that the King who is Judge of all is the crucified King and he is met in every one who suffers. It is because they had failed to understand Jesus' identification with the needy, the suffering, that the "goats" had failed to minister to him or to serve him. They had not loved the poor in concrete deeds of mercy. This Jesus, the crucified one, is the Son of man who utters judgment — but what kind of judgment is this? He is the one who identifies himself with the lowly — with all the daughters and sons of men. He is the loving and living expression of God's concern for humankind. A God bent on humankind, and nothing short of that, becomes the standard of our concern for those in need. That is why just this concern is the criterion of judgment. That is why the words of warning sound so harshly: "Depart from me, you cursed."

What matters is that we should see that seemingly irrevocable sentence against what we know of the God of the Old Testament and of the New. He is the wondrously inconsistent God who "grieves to his heart" that he ever had made this ornery human creature (Gen 6:5-8); he is the God whose heart "recoils within him" at the prospect of losing Ephraim (Hos 11:8); he is the God who desires the salvation of all (1 Tim 2:4); he is the God who did not spare his own Son (Jn 3:16). Surely Jesus would have us believe that his God and ours loves us with *divine* love that is beyond our human imagining.

Nothing of this is contradicted by that Matthean passage when one realises that the Last Judgment is *myth*. Though presented in the guise of an historical event it does not become irrelevant when one recognizes that its value is symbolic rather than historical. One is challenged to live in such a way that, should it occur, one would not be caught unawares. The "last judgment" is warning: it primarily relates to one's conduct in the present. While the King stresses his solidarity with "all," the exhortation is, by Matthew, addressed to Christians. We are being taught how we should prepare for the "coming" of the Lord, prepare for our meeting with him. Still, the universalist dimension remains. That is why I like, and make my own, a provocative comment on the Matthean judgment scene:

> I believe — and I say this with some hesitation — that at the last judgment perhaps everyone will stand at the right-hand side of the Son of Man: "Come all you beloved people, blessed of the Father, for despite all your inhumanity, you once gave a glass of water when I was in need. Come!"[4]

Does that seem outrageous? I do not think so. That man of Nazareth, who went about doing good, who died on a cross because he had espoused the cause of human freedom — he will not have us see God as an inflexible judge. He would have us see the tears of a God who weeps in concert with human woe.

[4]Edward Schillebeeckx, *God Among Us* (New York: Crossroad, 1983, 62).

6

THE TRIUMPH OF FAILURE

In some ways the painful Gethsemane episode is the most comforting in the gospels. There we see Jesus at his most human. Hitherto, he had gone resolutely to meet his fate. Now that the dreadful moment is upon him, "he began to be greatly distressed and troubled" (14:33) — it is almost impossible to convey adequately the force of Mark's Greek: Jesus is shattered.

It had been dawning on Jesus what it was the Father seemed to be asking of him. He needed to be assured that what God seemed to be asking he really did ask: "Abba, Father, all things are possible to you; remove this cup from me; yet not what I will but what you will" (14:36). This is the first and only time, in Mark's gospel, that Jesus is said to have spoken the Aramaic word "Abba" — the familiar title seems to be wrenched from him at this awful moment. He prays, explicitly, that the cup may be taken from him. He does not contemplate suffering and death with stoic calm.

Jesus does not want to die. He is appalled at the prospect: he knows fear. He is brave as he rises above his dread to embrace what it is God asks. But he must know if the path that opens before him is indeed the way that God would have him walk. He finds assurance in prayer: "And being in an agony he prayed more earnestly." His prayer did not go unanswered. As the epistle to the Hebrews puts it: "he was heard for his godly fear" (Heb 5:7). In traditional biblical imagery, Luke has dramatized the heavenly response: "And there appeared to him an angel from heaven strengthening him" (Lk 22:43). Jesus was assured that it was indeed the Father's will that he tread the lonely way of rejection. Not the Father's will as part of some cold inflexible design. No: he had understood that just here lay the victory over evil. For evil is finally helpless before a love that will never cry: Enough.

The Cry from the Cross

Gethsemane is a prelude to the anguished cry from the cross: "My God, my God, why have you forsaken me?" (Mk 15:34). Jesus suffers the absence of God: his cry of dereliction is just that, a cry of total desolation. The common explanation that the cry is the opening of Psalm 22, a psalm which ends on a confident note, is a factually true observation but makes nonsense of Mark's intent. He has Jesus die in total desolation, without any relieving feature at all. It would have seemed that, up to this point, Jesus' isolation could go no further: deserted by his disciples, taunted by his enemies, derided by those who hang with him, and suffocating in the darkness of evil. But the worst is now: abandoned by God. His suffering is radically lonely. Yet, his God is "my God." Even in this, as at Gethsemane, it is "not what I will, but what you will." Here, even more than then, the sheer humanness of Jesus is manifest. Now he knows what it means to give his life as a ransom for "many" (= all). Now the Son is wholly delivered into the hands of men. And the Father, too, in the Son, has abandoned himself to the humanity he would save — this is the deep meaning of that cry. The Father thereby holds out the gift of forgiveness to all who will recognize this vulnerable love.

The Challenge

The Triumph of Failure is the title of a novel by Canon Patrick Sheehan, a nineteenth century Irish parish priest who had quite a reputation as a novelist. I have, more than once, borrowed that title to describe the career of Jesus. Jesus was put to death. By the standards of the world he was a failure. True, he had got off to a promising start in his acknowledged task of renewing Israel and had won a heartening response. But, as Peter showed at Caesarea Philippi, those who had begun to pin vague or more explicit messianic expectations on him quickly became disillusioned — what was all this about suffering and death? (Mk 8:27-33). The poignant words of the two Emmaus disciples are eloquent: "We had hoped that he was the one to redeem Israel!" (Lk 24:21) — they had been let down with a bang.

Failure is an inescapable factor of our human existence. Too often, God knows, our failure may be blameworthy. But there is much failure beyond our control. Surely it would be a comfort, in our times of failure, to know that Jesus, too, had had a real experience of failure. We recall the consoling word of Hebrews: "Because he himself has suffered and been tempted, he is able to help those who are tempted" (Heb 2:18). Surely it is heartening, in the dejection of failure, to hear in the silence of prayer, the gentle, reassuring words: "My sister, my brother, I too knew the agony of failure." But to hear these words we must first be prepared to acknowledge a Jesus who could fail. If our christology will not allow for that — then he can be no real help to us in our times of failure.

"If we mean to honor God's saving purpose we shall submit to the judgment of the man Jesus; only then will we acquire an outlook upon the living God ... To put it starkly: whereas God is bent on showing himself in human form, we on our side slip past this human aspect as quickly as we can in order to admire a 'divine ikon' from which every trait of the critical prophet has been smoothed away."[1] This expresses, so well, something that I have long felt. We had indeed put Jesus back where he came from. And wisely, because we had realized, a long time ago, that he is much safer there! We genuflect toward "Our Divine Lord" —who does not impinge on us because, as we thus envisage him, he does not really have any critical impact on the life of our world. But Jesus of Nazareth is a very uncomfortable person to have around. Try listening — and I mean really *listen* — to any of his parables and you will see what I mean. In his

---

[1]Edward Schillebeeckx, *Jesus.* An Experiment in Christology. (New York: Crossroad, 1981, 671).

own life-style and his words he is a challenge. In all he said and in all he did he bore witness to a Father bent on the salvation of humankind. The snag is that he expects us to reflect God's concern for us in our concern for one another. And that we do not like. But the fact remains that salvation has to be within our human world. If it comes from outside, then God is no more than a magician, waving a magic wand. God is not a magician but the God of loving concern for his exasperating human children. Through his Son Jesus he enters into every human hurt that is not sin — and through the sinless Jesus he touches and heals the hurt that is sin. Through the failure of his beloved Son he transforms our failures.

Experience of Failure

The crucial question is: did Jesus see and experience crucifixion as the failure of his plans? I believe that the answer is: yes. Of course, one must be clear as to what his plan was. Here, as much as anywhere, we must cut through the layers of New Testament christology and, much more so, of later christology. We should recall that if the apostles preached Jesus, Jesus had proclaimed the rule of God. We must be clear that Jesus did not come to establish a *new* Israel. His call was to *metanoia*, to a radical change of heart; he had come to *renew* Israel. A surely authentic word of Jesus (because it must have been embarrassing for a church that had turned to the Gentiles) is the declaration: "I was sent only to the lost sheep of the house of Israel" (Mt 15:24; cf 10:6). He had come to summon Israel to become what God wanted his people to be. His life had been spent in that task. Now, popular disillusionment and official rejection had frustrated that task; sentence of death had brought it to a jarring halt. He can no longer preach the rule of God. Though he was in no way responsible for it, and had done everything to avoid failure, he was draining the bitter dregs of failure. There, I believe, is another dimension of the anguished cry: "My God, my God, why have you forsaken me?"

Jesus came to bear witness to a God bent on humankind. Now he entrusts his experience of failure to God. He, like us, had to reconcile a painful experience of failure with this trust in God. For the synoptists, and especially Mark, show that in no way did Jesus begin his mission with a vision of violent death at the end of the road. And if at a later stage he had to face the fact that violent death was the likely issue, we have seen, in our look at the Gethsemane episode, that he still did not fully understand God's way — but filially bowed to the Father's will. His Gethsemane decision was to trust in God despite the darkness of his situation.

Triumph of Failure

The fact remains that "for Jesus his violent death was *historically* a fiasco."[2] What is implied is a distinction between the terms "historical" and "historic." One can label "historical" anything that happens in history. An "historic" event is a happening of far-reaching historical significance.

[2]Edward Schillebeeckx, *Christ.* The Experience of Jesus as Lord. (New York: Crossroad, 1981, 829).

The truth of the matter is that his death marked Jesus as *historically* a failure. Jesus was executed on the order of a Roman provincial official: an alleged troublemaker in that bothersome province of Judea had been dealt with. The incident did not raise a ripple in imperial affairs. Yet history has shown that this execution was an event of *historic* proportions. Its ripples flow stronger than ever two thousand years later.

Let us be clear about it. The Romans and the Jewish sanhedrin had effectively closed the "Jesus case." The aims and message of Jesus, and his life itself, had ended in death. His prophetic voice had been muzzled. That is failure. The question is: *Why* had Jesus been silenced? It was because he, unflinchingly, had lived and preached God's love for humankind. That is why he had tablefellowship with sinners, why he sought to free men and women from the tyranny of religion, why he, at every hand's turn, bore witness to the true God. He might, in face of the threatening opposition, have packed up and gone home to Nazareth. That would have been *real* failure. But he would not be turned from witnessing to God's love. They might take his life — but to his last breath he would witness. "Father, forgive them" —there is the victory. What Jesus tells us is that failure is *not* the last word — that is, as God views failure.

From God's point of view, in the fate of Jesus, there can be no talk of failure. This is what John brings out, dramatically, in his gospel. He undoubtedly knew the synoptic tradition (though not the Synoptic Gospels) but he chose to turn their tragedy into comedy. What is important for us in his presentation is that he has understood what the others imply:

failure is not the last word. But what Mark has done is at least of equal importance: he has shown that a sense of failure, even for Jesus, is a grievous human experience.

There is a further point. Too often the resurrection of Jesus is presented as a rescue operation. As someone has put it graphically: it is like the close of a Western movie when the beleaguered pioneer wagon train is saved by a troop of U.S. cavalry riding out of the sunset. The truth is that resurrection is inherent in the life and death of Jesus. His "failure" was his total commitment to God and to human-kind. That historical moment of failure on the cross was God's overcoming of human failure. If Paul can declare of the Christian that nothing in all creation can separate him or her from the love of God (Rom 8:39), a death motivated only by love cannot, for a moment, cut off Jesus from his God. The human cry of God-forsakenness ("My God, my God why have you forsaken me?" — (Mk 15:34) is heavy with *feeling*. The reality is quite other: never were Son and Father more wholly one. The ultimate helplessness of death was disclosed. "God raised him up, having loosed the pangs of death, *because it was not possible for him to be held by it*" (Acts 2:24).

Like Us in Every Respect

Another New Testament writer who had come to terms, theologically, with the death of Jesus, was the author of the letter to the Hebrews. He has thoroughly understood that the salvation of humankind cannot be a salvation *from* humanness but *in* our humanness. Salvation from outside would be no salvation. What has come to pass is something intensely moving: God, in Jesus, reaching into our history of suffering and brokenness. "It was fitting that he, from whom and by whom all things exist, in bringing many children to glory, should make the pioneer of their salvation perfect through suffering" (Heb 2:10). God has made our cause his concern.

Our human history, before the *eschaton*, [the End], is one largely compounded of suffering and unrighteousness. It is therefore "appropriate" (Heb 2:10) — in accordance with the character of our God — that in seeking to bring human-kind to "glory," the destined End, in and through Jesus, he should have Jesus walk the road of human suffering. He has become one of us, sharing our sorrow and our anxiety, in order to be the first to reach perfection — the first to become the true image of God, the first to become wholly human. It is fitting indeed that we, trapped in a history of suffering, should be set free by one who has entered into that suffering and made it his own (2:10). We can truly see God in the face of Jesus.

For the author of Hebrews Jesus is Son of God; but he is the Son who "had to be made like his brethren in every respect" (2:17), a Son who "in every respect has been tempted as we are, yet without sinning" (4:15). He is the human being who stands in a relationship of obedient faithfulness towards God (3:16) and who stands in solidarity with human suffering. Thereby he is mediator: a true priest who can bring human-kind to God. If he bears "the very stamp of God's nature" (1:3) it is because we see in him what makes God God; he shows us that God is God of humankind.

The author is surely aware of the pattern of the life of Jesus — there are several pointers throughout his homily. But, like Paul, he concentrates on the moment of death (and exaltation): he finds the meaning of the life of Jesus in his crucifixion — accepted as a self-sacrifice for broken humankind. He had come to do the saving will of the Father and had learned God's purpose in the "school of suffering" (5:8). In Gethsemane he had prayed "with loud cries and tears to him who was able to save him from death" (5:7); he came to understand that the way of faithfulness led to the cross.

The death of Jesus is presented as a bloody sacrifice; the accent is on Jesus' self-surrender in this violent death. (One might remark, in passing, how perverse it is that later theology tended to explain the death of Jesus in terms of Old Testament sacrifice — while Hebrews is singlemindedly concerned to demonstrate that our High Priest has transcended and replaced the whole Old Testament cultic system. We thereby made so many difficulties for ourselves). Because the sacrifice is the death of Jesus it marked the end of his earthly life. Yet, the sacrifice of Jesus did not end on the cross. By God's graciousness (2:9) his death was for the benefit of all men and women. The Father had seen in the death of Jesus the supreme assertion of his love for humankind and his faithfulness towards God — for we must always have in mind that the meaning of Jesus' death is to be found in his life. Exaltation to the right hand of the Father is the divine recognition of the significance of the death of Jesus, giving this death its abiding, eternal value.

He Has Risen

It is clear, from the New Testament, that Christians were, from the first, convinced that the crucified Jesus was not held by death. In Jewish faith and prayer, God is he who "makes the dead live." Jewish faith and hope looked to a resurrection of the righteous at the end of time. What the first Christians asserted was that, in the person of Jesus of Nazareth, this divine act had taken place. Jewish expectation was eschatological: resurrection was an event of the End-time. Christians asserted that an eschatological event had taken place in time. If one can put it so, the resurrection of Jesus is an event at once eschatological and historical. It is a spiritual event, beyond our world of time, and yet it has impinged on our world of time.

Six gospel passages serve as sources for our knowledge of the resurrection: Mk 16:1-8; Mt 28; Lk 24:13-49; Jn 20; Jn 21; Mk 16:9-20 (and to these should be added Paul's text in 1 Cor 15:5-8). In this group we may distinguish two types of narrative: those of post-resurrection appearances and those of the finding of the empty tomb. The narratives of the post-resurrection appearances were composed to ground christian faith in the risen Jesus and to justify apostolic preaching. The nature of such appearances make it obvious enough that the gospels cannot agree where and to whom Jesus appeared. This diversity does not seriously effect the historicity of the events; it is a product of the way in which the stories were told and preserved. A basic pattern is followed when Jesus is said to appear to the Twelve (eleven). The disciples are together and are apprehensive. Jesus appears, is at first unrecognized, and ends by giving a solemn command, which includes the commission to carry to humankind the good news of Jesus and his gift of salvation. Each gospel witness stresses some particular appearance or some significant aspect of one, and each evangelist has presented his material in the light of his own theological interest. We may think of Luke's memorable account of the appearances on the road to Emmaus (24:13-27), or John's moving picture of Jesus standing on the lake shore and inviting the disciples to have breakfast with him (21:4-14).

The Tomb

The empty tomb figures in our earliest gospel version of the resurrection-story. Mark relates that the women —Mary Magdalene, Mary the mother of James, and Salome —intent on anointing the body of Jesus, came to the tomb early on the first day of the week. To their surprise they found the great stone already rolled back (16:1-4). Entering the tomb they were amazed to find a young man dressed in white sitting there. He said to them, "Do not be amazed; you seek Jesus of Nazareth, who was crucified. He has risen, he is not here; see the place where they laid him" (16:5-6). The "young man" plays the role of *angelus interpres*, of interpreting angel, a feature of apocalyptic. The women were faced with the riddle of an empty tomb; he explains why the tomb is empty. It is a neat literary way of presenting, as economically as possible, the fact of the empty tomb and the reason for its emptiness. Mark may be the earliest of our gospel texts but, as we shall see, later texts than it have preserved traces of more primitive tradition.

In Matthew 28:1-8 the two Marys come "to see the sepulchre"; they could do no more because, for Matthew, the tomb is sealed and under guard (27:62-66). Already, at the death of Jesus, Matthew had introduced an earthquake ("and the earth shook, and the rocks were split," 27:51) to signify God's judgment on the old age. This other "great earthquake" of 28:2 links the resurrection with the death as the eschatological event which ushers in the new age. Here the "young man" of Mark is an awe-inspiring "angel of the Lord" (18:4), but his message to the women is the same (18:5-6; cf. Mk 16:6). While Matthew has other important motifs, he has not advanced our understanding of the empty tomb.

Luke breaks fresh ground (24:1-12). He explicitly records failure to find the body. The women ("Mary Magdalene and Joanna and Mary the mother of James and the other women with them," 24:10) had come, as in Mark, to anoint the body. While they puzzled over the absence of the body of "the Lord Jesus" (v.3), "two young men stood by them in dazzling apparel" (v.5) — a fascinating development of Mark's "young man" and Matthew's "angel of the Lord." The "two men" challenge the women's concern with the tomb: why are you seeking the living one in this place of the dead? (v.5). In vv.6-8 we have a striking example of Luke's editorial freedom. Since, in his theological plan, the climax of his gospel must be in Jerusalem he cannot, without bringing about an anti-climax, record apparitions in Galilee. So he rewrites Mark 16:7 and changes the promise of an appearance in Galilee into a prophecy made by Jesus "while he was still in Galilee." Again, unlike the women of Mark who "said nothing to any one" (Mk 16:8), the women in Luke "told all this to the eleven and to all the rest" (Lk 24:9). The apostles, however, set no store by this "idle tale" (v.11). Verse 12 offers one of the many contacts with the Johannine tradition evident in Luke's passion and resurrection narrative. It tells that Peter went hastily to the tomb, saw the linen cloths (which had wrapped the body of Jesus) lying there, and came away, quite puzzled (cf Lk 24:22-24).

John has preserved two versions of the women's visit to the tomb — 20:1-3 and 11-13. Underlying the first of them (vv. 1-2) would seem to be the earliest form of an empty tomb narrative in any gospel: "Now on the first day of the week Mary Magdalene came to the tomb early, while it was still dark, and saw that the stone had been taken away from the tomb. So she ran, and went to Simon Peter and the other disciple, the one whom Jesus loved and said to them, 'They have taken the Lord out of the tomb, and we do not know where they have laid him'" (Jn 20:1-2). John has introduced the Beloved Disciple and has, for his own dramatic purpose, reduced the original group of women to Mary Magdalene, preparing the way for the later christophany to her (vv. 14-18). It is this christophany, and not an angelic spokesman, which explains the meaning of the empty tomb (vv.12-13). But the tradition which he has thus rewritten is early indeed.

Thoroughly Johannine is 20:3-10. At Mary Magdalene's disturbing news (v. 2), Peter and "the other disciples" hurry to the tomb. In the tradition, Peter's companion was unnamed. John has introduced him as the Beloved Disciple so that his coming to faith might interpret the significance of the empty tomb. The burial cloths and, more especially, their arrangement, are a sign that Mary's interpretation of the empty tomb ("they have taken the Lord out of the tomb," 20:2) is not the correct one. Jesus has not been "taken" anywhere. Rather he has left mortality behind him. Only the Beloved Disciple (20:2-8), seeing the sign, believes — "he saw and believed" (v.8). Manifestly, he believes not merely in the woman's word but even before any appearance of the risen Lord — and from an understanding of the scriptures (20:9) — in the risen Christ himself. It is as if this faith is less the result of human effort and understanding than the effect of Christ's love within the disciple. And this is surely John's intent because, while the "Beloved Disciple" is a real person and the source of John's tradition, he also represents the christian disciple who is sensitive, in faith and love, to the presence of the risen Jesus. With this one (theological) exception of the Beloved Disciple who saw with eyes of faith, the "empty tomb" is never regarded as a reason for faith in the resurrection but always as a confirming sign. That Jesus can no longer be found in the tomb because he is risen (and not for any other reason) can only be the object of faith.

He Showed Himself

In 1 Corinthians 15 Paul energetically defends the reality of resurrection from the dead. He starts by appealing to the resurrection of Jesus and quotes an early creed: "Christ died for our sins according to the scriptures and he was buried and was raised on the third day according to the scriptures, and he appeared to Cephas, then to the Twelve" (15:3-5).

The statement, "he was buried" underlines the reality of Jesus' death. The statement "he appeared to" expresses the conviction of the first Christians that Jesus had returned to the stage of history. Paul (vv. 6-7) adds a series of witnesses not mentioned in the gospels and ends (v.8) with his own experience on the road to Damascus. Significantly, he makes no distinction between the appearance to himself and the appearances to the other witnesses. Interestingly, when Luke takes up the Damascus-road story, as he does three times (Acts 9:1-19; 22:4-16; 26:9-18), never once does he declare that Paul actually saw Jesus. What he saw was "a light from heaven" (9:3; 22:6; 26:13); what he heard was a voice speaking to him (9:4; 22:7; 26:14). Evidently, Luke does not think it necessary that a real encounter with the risen Lord — and Paul's was surely a real encounter — should involve a visual encounter.

Paul uses the verb *ōphthē* to state that Jesus appeared to Cephas, to the other witnesses listed, and to Paul himself —"he appeared to Cephas, then to the Twelve. Then he appeared to more than five hundred brethren at one time . . . Then he appeared to James, then to all the apostles. Last of all . . . he appeared to me" (1 Cor 15:5-8). The word can be rendered "he showed himself." It means that the risen Jesus manifested himself as present in some fashion so that Paul, and the others, can say, "I have seen the Lord." What is involved is a divine initiative leading to a real experience of the presence of the Lord and a firm conviction of the reality of this presence. But how can one talk about resurrection from the dead? Never is there any attempt to describe the resurrection because it was realized that it is a happening beyond our experience. Only symbol and imagery, not literal prose, could tell *this* story. Something had happened to these men and women which they could only describe by saying they had "seen the Lord" — that he had "shown himself" to them. The phrase did not refer to some general christian experience but rather to a particular series of occurrences confined to a limited period. Such occurrences, on the threshold of ordinary human experience, just would not submit to precision of detail. "The original witnesses were *dead sure* that they had met with Jesus, and there was not more to be said about it."[3]

Apologetics

A constant feature of the resurrection narratives, with the exception of Matthew 28:8-10, is that the Lord is not at once recognized (Lk 24:16, 37; Jn 20:14-15; 21:4); it required some word or familiar gesture of his to make him known. This is an effective way of making the point that Jesus had not returned to life as before but had passed beyond death, to *new* life with God. He is Jesus — and yet he is different. The appearance stories are heavily laden with theological and apologetic motifs.

At the appearance of Jesus to the eleven and to the couple who had hurried back from Emmaus, all present "were startled and frightened and supposed that they saw a spirit" (Lk 24:36). Jesus invites them to see and feel his hands and feet and he eats in their presence (24:39-43). The apologetic concern is obvious: Jesus shows that he is, in his new state,

[3]C.H. Dodd, *The Founder of Christianity* (London: Collins, 1971, 170).

the same person they had known prior to the crucifixion. The assertion that he invited touching of his (wounded) hands and feet and that he ate before them, is in the apologetic of the day, a firm christian rejection of any challenge to the reality of the new life of their Lord (cf Jn 20:25, 27; 21:9).

In Matthew, the sealing and guarding of the tomb (27:62-66) is clearly a christian counter to a Jewish charge that the body of Jesus had been stolen by his disciples, who could then claim that he was risen and had been seen by them. The christian retort was that the Jews and Romans had conspired to prevent just that eventuality but that God had had his way despite their efforts. And they went on the attack by claiming that the accusation of grave-robbery was, in the first place, a lie propagated by the Jewish authorities precisely to cover-up the embarrassing fact of resurrection (28:11-15). All of this is a technique — acceptable at the time — of rebutting an accusation that is *known* to be false. An intriguing point is that the obvious counter to resurrection, that the body is still in the tomb, seems not to have been made. At any rate these later details — guarded tomb, display of wounds, eating — are apologetic arguments, not hard facts. The hard face is the christian conviction that the Lord *is* risen. God, and not death, has the last word.

7

A RESPECTABLE JESUS

Jesus was too much for his contemporaries — and especially for the religious people of his day. It is not very surprising that he met opposition from them. In their eyes, his was not the proper conduct of a "man of God." The company he kept was disreputable. He challenged their fondly-held traditions. His God was hardly recognizable as their God. It would have been bad enough if all of this had involved only himself. What was intolerable was that Jesus had a following. His way had an appeal. The time came when he had to be stopped.

It must be acknowledged that Jesus was not very "prudent." He was casually unconventional. He welcomed women among his entourage. Even his own disciples were taken aback by his encounter with a lone woman at Jacob's well (Jn 4:27). They were equally nonplussed by his regard for children: "And they were bringing children to him, that he might touch them, and the disciples rebuked them. But when Jesus saw it he was indignant . . . and he took them in his arms and blessed them, laying his hands upon them" (Mk 10:13-14, 16; cf 9:36). The unctious flattery of the Pharisees as they baited a trap for Jesus is heavy with irony. "Teacher, we know that you are true, and care for no man, for you do not regard the position of men, but truly teach the way of God" (Mk 12:14).

Jesus was not a schooled rabbi and yet had a small inner coterie of disciples whom he taught — but not in rabbinical lore. In any case, the Twelve were not rabbinical material, rather they were of the despised *am-ha-aretz* (the "people of the land"). For that matter, one of them was a tax-collector! It had to be expected that those who listened to him were the ignorant. "Have any of the authorities or of the Pharisees believed in him? But this crowd who do not know the law, are accursed" (Jn 7:48-49).

What hurt most of all was that Jesus, who had never avoided encounter with the Pharisees, was forthright in his criticism of them. That is evident in his parables. The Pharisees did not enjoy being told that "God rejoices more over one sinner who repents that over ninety-nine righteous person who need no repentance" (Lk 15:7; cf 15:10). In the same chapter the elder son in the parable of 15:11-31 is a mirror held up to the Pharisees: they are scandalized by the forgiving love of God. Again in Luke there is the parable of the Pharisee and the Tax Collector with the thoroughly unacceptable verdict that it was the prayer of the "sinner" which won a hearing and not the prayer of the righteous Pharisee (18:14). And, in the Good Samaritan, when pointedly asked: "Which of these three, do you think, proved neighbor to the man who fell among the robbers?"

the scribe must answer: "The one who showed mercy to him" — though he be a despised Samaritan (10:36-37). Jesus never shrank from challenging his opponents.

Like Us in All Things?

The point I seek to make in this chapter is that Christians, too, before long began to find Jesus — that thoroughly human Jesus — rather too much. They began to decide how Jesus ought to have acted. Manifestly, their faith in him as risen Lord was influencing, perhaps unconsciously, their assessment of his humanness. We can illustrate the point simply enough and clearly enough by comparing some passages of Mark with parallel passages of Matthew and/or Luke.

In Mark we read that "Jesus came from Nazareth of Galilee and was baptized by John in the Jordan" (1:9) — he was one of a crowd awaiting baptism. Matthew was evidently embarrassed by the episode and rewrote it: Jesus came to be baptized but "John would have prevented him, saying, 'I need to be baptized by you, and do you come to me?' But Jesus answered him 'Let it be so now; for thus it is fitting for us to fulfill all righteousness.' Then he consented" (Mt 3:13-15). The tradition that Jesus had been baptized by John might not be denied, but it could be made more "edifying." Luke, with his interest in the Holy Spirit, had turned the story into one of bestowal of the Spirit: "When Jesus also had been baptized and was praying, the heaven was opened, and the Holy Spirit descended upon him in bodily form, as a dove" (Lk 3:21-22).

At the incident of the healing of a man on the sabbath Jesus reacted to the hostile silence that met his demand: "Is it lawful on the sabbath to do good or to do harm, to save life or to kill?" — "And he looked around at them with anger, grieved at their hardness of heart" (Mk 3:4-5). This becomes in Luke: "And he looked around on them all" (Lk 6:10), while Matthew omits all reference to grief or angry look (Mt 12:9-14). In the episode of the children Matthew (19;13-15) and Luke (18:15-17) carefully refrain from saying that Jesus took them in his arms (cf Mk 9:36; 10:16); seemingly, they would regard such intimacy as not in good taste.

There is the Gethsemane event with Mark's painful emphasis on Jesus' suffering and his version of the prayer with its admission that Jesus, even at this late stage, could hope to escape the "hour" (Mk 14:33-36). Unexpected is the Lucan observation: "And there appeared to him an angel from heaven, strengthening him. And being in an agony he prayed more earnestly; and his sweat became like great drops of blood falling down upon the ground" (Lk 22:43-44). It is no surprise that later scribes found the passage offensive and the verses are missing from many manuscripts of Luke. Far more tellingly we find that in the Fourth Gospel Gethsemane has been radically reinterpreted. In what is assuredly an allusion to the Gethsemane prayer the Johannine Jesus asserts:

> Now is my soul troubled. And what shall I say, "Father save me from this hour?" No, for this purpose I came to this hour (Jn 12:27).

Obviously, we have reached a new stage in a "revisionary" portrayal of Jesus.

The Johannine Jesus

This brings us to the Fourth Gospel. It does not need long to recognize that the Johannine Jesus is, in many respects, quite different from the Jesus of the synoptists. In the synoptics Jesus message concerns "the kingdom of God," the benevolent rule of God. In John what Jesus preaches, what he reveals, is himself. Jesus is still concerned to make the real God known, but now who God is can be known and seen in Jesus himself: "No one has ever seen God, the only Son, who is in the bosom of the Father, he has made him known" (Jn 1:18). There is a whole series of "I am" sayings — "I am the bread of life" (6:35, 51); "I am the light of the world" (8:12); "I am the good shepherd" (10:11, 14); "I am the resurrection and the life" (11:25); "I am the way, and the truth and the life" (14:6).

All along Jesus is making claims about himself which are equivalent to claims made directly or indirectly of Yahweh in the Old Testament. This reaches its height in the four absolute "I AM" sayings: "You will die in your sins unless you believe that I AM." "When you have lifted up (in crucifixion) the Son of man, then you will know that I AM"; "Before Abraham was I AM"; " . . . that you may believe that I AM" (8:24, 28, 58; 13:19). Each time there is a conscious echo of the divine name of Exodus 3:14, in the word to Moses; "say this to the people of Israel, I AM has sent me to you." We should not lose sight of the fact that the one who speaks of himself as the "I AM" also declares, unambiguously, "The Father is greater than I" (14:28).

The Johannine Jesus harps continually on his relationship to the Father: "God so loved the world that he gave his only

Son" (3:16); "he whom God has sent utters the words of God" (3:34); "the Father loves the Son and shows him all that he himself is doing" (5:20); "the Father judges no one but has given all judgment to the Son" (5:22); "he who does not honor the Son does not honor the Father who sent him" (5:23); "as the Father has life in himself, so he has granted the Son also to have life in himself" (5:26); "if you knew me, you would know my Father also" (8:19); "I and the Father are one" (10:30). The question stares us in the face: why this remarkable contrast with the synoptic tradition? For, while we may have declared the synoptic Jesus to be the one who defines God, the Johannine Revealer seems to be well-nigh identical with God.

A Claim Too Far?

Recent studies on the Johannine writings[1] have uncovered evidence of christological turmoil within the Johannine communities which served to foment their distinctive christological development. The first Johannine Christians were, all of them, Jews who lived within the synagogue structure. They acknowledged Jesus as the fulfillment of Israel's hope, a hope enshrined in Israel's Scriptures. He had been foreseen by Moses and the Prophets (Jn 1:45;5:39;7:52). They acclaimed him under the titles Messiah (1:41;4:25-26,29;7:26),

---

[1]To mention only two scholars: Raymond E. Brown, *The Gospel According to John* [Anchor Bible] (New York: Doubleday, 1966, 1971); *The Epistles of John* [AB] (New York: Doubleday, 1982); and Jerome Neyrey, *Christ Is Community: The Christologies of the New Testament* (Wilmington, DE: M. Glazier, 1985).

King of Israel (1:49;12:13-15), Son of God (1:49). With conviction and emphasis they proclaimed their faith before their fellow Jews.

Before long these followers of Jesus came to realize that their claims for him could no longer be contained within the wineskin of traditional Judaism. The Jesus who had been announced by Moses and the Prophets had, in fact, replaced Moses and the Prophets. They maintained that Jesus was immeasurably superior to all of the religious figures of Israel. In debate with their "orthodox" brethren they tended to push their claims further and more sharply. As the unique Revealer, Jesus is *the* Word of God (1:1). He and he alone had seen the true God (1:18;6:46); those whom Scripture had asserted to have seen God had, in fact, seen Jesus (8:56). For, Jesus is "equal to God" (5:18;10:33) and can assume the name of God: I AM (8:24,28,58;13:19). We do not know how far the synagogue might have stretched, but there had to be a "bottom line." Such claims had reached and passed that bottom line. From now on, one must be a Jew *or* a Christian. In the Johannine community, as in the early christian communities in general, the tragic moment was when Christianity broke free of its roots — perhaps, more accurately, when Judaism could no longer tolerate the disciples of Jesus of Nazareth.

The history of the Johannine community reminds us that there are always two sides to a story. For an orthodox Jew those Johannine Christians were hard to take; a breaking-point was reached. The most sacred dogma of the religion of Judaism was its firm monotheism: " Hear, O Israel: the Lord our God is one Lord" (Dt 6:4) — enshrined in the daily prayer called the Shema (= "Hear") from the opening word of the deuteronomic credo. Now, however, these Johannine Christians were making their Jesus equal to God. That is the point of the accusations: "you, being a man, make yourself God" (10:33) and "he made himself equal to God" (5:18). A Thomas could hail the risen Jesus as "My Lord and my God" (20:28). What were orthodox Jews to think? Surely this was a body-blow to monotheism, an assertion that there was another God side by side with Yahweh. And it has to be acknowledged that the doctrine of the Trinity, as popularly understood, must seem to Judaism and Islam a denial of monotheism. At any rate, however precisely the Johannine Christians understood their claims, the same claims were heresy to their Jewish brothers and sisters. Hence, "the Jews" who figure throughout the Fourth Gospel are the "unbelievers" who will not accept the Johannine Christ.

This Is a Hard Saying

Things began to go very badly wrong for Johannine Christians. In the first place, they found themselves excommunicated from the synagogue. In chapter 9 of John the parents of the man born blind will not be drawn into the quarrel "because they feared the Jews, for the Jews had already agreed that if any one should confess him to be Christ, he was to be put out of the synagogue" (9:22;cf 9:34). The same evidence emerges from 12:42 — "Many even of the authorities believed in him, but for fear of the Pharisees they did not confess it, lest they should be put out of the synagogue," and from 16:2 — "They will put you out of the synagogues; indeed the hour is coming when whoever kills you will think he is offering service to God."

While this persecution might be stoically borne by the group, the further fact that many of their number baulked at what they judged to be the unacceptable implications of the developed christology was a bitter pill to swallow. This emerges in chapter 6. There were those who believed in Jesus because of his "signs" (6:14,26). Now they found the claim that he was the "one come down from heaven" (6:38,41) to be too much to take. Their objection is explicit in 6:42 — "Is not this Jesus, the son of Joseph, whose father and mother we know? How does he now say, 'I have come down from heaven'." Furthermore, he is the one who alone has seen God (6:46), the one who alone can give eternal life (6:40). All these claims had been made before: a heavenly descending figure (1:14;3:3) who alone had seen God (1:18), giver of eternal life (5:21-22).

Here, in chapter 6, what is noteworthy is the reaction of *disciples*: "Many of his disciples, when they heard it, said, This is a hard saying; who can listen to it?" The question, "Do you take offense at this?" (6:61) must be answered in light of the following comment: "What if you were to see the Son of man ascending where he was before?" (6:62). Evidently, offense is taken at the claim that Jesus was a descended heavenly being.[2]

"After this many of his disciples went back and no longer went about with him" (6:66). The Johannine community,

---

[2]The objection voiced in 6:60-66 should be taken in relation to 6:35-50 (rather than in relation to 6:51-58). See R.E. Brown, *The Gospel According to John I-XII*, 299-303.

already troubled at excommunication from the synagogue, was severely shaken by the "desertion" of many of their number.

The reaction of those who remained was predictable: they further hardened their christological stance. For one thing, their emphasis on Jesus as one "descended" from the heavenly world came to mean that he was "not of this world" (cf 17:16). (A corollary was that the community, too, saw itself as not really of the world.) Emphasis on the otherworldliness of Jesus meant that the significance of Jesus' life and death became obscured — a fact that surfaces in the Johannine Letters. We have observed that the high christological claims were wholly unacceptable to traditional Jews fighting for survival after the debacle of the Jewish-Roman war of 66-70 A.D. Lines of orthodoxy were now firmly drawn and "heresy" could not be tolerated.

There were Johannine Christians for whom their monotheistic faith seemed threatened by the same claims — a "hard saying" which they were unable to accept. In face of expulsion and desertion the core group stuck to its guns:

> The confession of Jesus as a heavenly figure becomes the touchstone of authentic membership. It becomes, in fact, required for salvation, "Unless you believe that 'I AM,' you will die in your sins" (8:24). The emotional and social value of the confession of Jesus as a heavenly figure has been affected by the excommunication. It is the only, best and necessary confession. And it functions to separate the Johannine group from the synagogue and to distinguish authentic believers from pseudo-believers within the group."[3]

[3]Jerome Neyrey, *op. cit.*, 179.

Schism

The high christological confession had served to distinguish authentic Johannine believers from those now regarded as pseudo-believers. But the matter was far from settled. The Johannine Letters tell of a further schism — again over the christological issue. In 1 John 2:18 the author, using apocalyptic language, asserts that the appearance of "antichrists" signals the "last hour." It is disturbing to learn, in the next verse, who these "antichrists" are: "They went out from us, but they were not of us; for if they had been of us, they would have continued with us; but they went out, that it might be plain that all were not of us" (2:19) — the "antichrists" are none other than those Johannine Christians who have broken with the author's party.[4]

It is abundantly clear that the reason for the split was christological. In 2 John 7 we have the equivalent of the "antichrist" text of 1 John 2:19 — "For many deceivers have gone out into the world, men who will not acknowledge the coming of Jesus Christ in the flesh; such a one is the deceiver and the antichrist." In contrast stand the true believers who "confess that Jesus Christ has come in the flesh" — and who can make that confession because they possess the Spirit of God, not the spirit of antichrist (1 Jn 4:2-3). Manifestly, the

---

[4]The Johannine Letters illustrate all too sadly that charity is the first victim of fraternal polemic. These former brethren are now not only antichrists but haters of the brethren (1:9-11), murderers like Cain (3:12), children of the devil (3:8-10), they belong to the faithless world (4:5). Hence, the true believers will have nothing to do with them (2 Jn 10). The author of the Letters, who stresses love so, tends to be singularly unloving when it comes to those whom he regarded as deserters.

issue is "come in the flesh." This does not at all mean a denial of incarnation — the "secessionists" (a convenient term for the breakaway group) are not docetists. The trouble with the secessionists is that they had pushed high christology a stage further. For them the entry of the heavenly figure into our world — the Word-made-flesh — was, in itself, the saving event; the life and death of Jesus had no saving significance. They took their stand on an interpretation of the Johannine tradition — which the author of the Letters regarded as misinterpretation.[5] He insists on the saving importance of the life and death of Jesus. That is what he asserts when he declares: "This he who came by water and blood, Jesus Christ, not with the water only but with the water and the blood" (1 Jn 5:6). The sense of the enigmatic language is obvious enough when seen in a Johannine environment. It might seem that the first manifestation of the Word-made-flesh, at his baptism, was enough. After all, John the Baptist had declared: "I saw the Spirit descend as a dove from heaven, and it remained on him" (Jn 1:32): Jesus was, at that moment, *fully* revealed as the Christ, the Son of God. The author refers to the crucifixion-scene of 19:34-35: the flow of blood and water from the side of the dead Jesus. *This* was the moment when the saving Spirit was poured out (7:38-39). In other words, the death of Jesus was a saving event. Indeed, the whole earthly career of Jesus has saving significance: that is what it means to confess "Jesus Christ come in flesh." And there is where the secessionists had gone wrong.

[5]That this is the meaning of "come in the flesh" and that all the secessionist positions follow on a particular interpretation of Johannine data has been brilliantly and convincingly argued by R.E. Brown in his *The Epistles of John.*

Johannine Christology

Up to this chapter we have presented, in the main, the Jesus to be discerned behind Mark. What of the Jesus of John? If one, for instance, compares the Marcan and Johannine passion narratives (Mk 14:43-15:47; Jn 18:2-19:42) one has to conclude that they are, in several respects, historically irreconcilable. One may note, for instance, the descriptions of the arrest (Mk 14:43-52; Jn 18:2-11) or, again, silence before Pilate on the one side and a spirited dialogue on the other (Mk 15:1-5; Jn 18:28-10:16). And there is the death: life crushed from a shattered Jesus (Mk 15:33-37) or a serene Jesus calmly choosing the moment of his death (Jn 19:28-30). Of course, the contrast is there right from the start of the two gospels. There is no doubt about the humanness of the man of Nazareth who was baptized by John (Mk 1:9). It is the majestic Word-made-flesh who strides through the pages of John. Admittedly, his Jesus can be found sitting wearily by a well (Jn 4:6); he is the man who "loved Martha and her sister and Lazarus" (11:5) and who wept at the death of his friend (11:35). But these are rare flashes. Johannine christology has to be approached with the greatest care.

All things considered, it was unfortunate that this christology had gained almost total dominance during the fateful christological debates of the fourth-fifth centuries. For all its brilliance and its attractiveness the Johannine christology cries out for balance. It needs, above all, the balance of the *theologia crucis* of Mark and Paul. There is a seductive quality about the Johannine outlook which tends to blind one to its shortcomings. It is not without significance that, historically, the Fourth Gospel quickly became popular in Gnostic circles. While there is no Gnosticism in John, its language, unlike that of the synoptics, lent itself to Gnostic interpretation. For that reason the gospel was suspect in the early church. The irony is that, once accepted, its christology soon held sway.

Neither this chapter nor the whole first part of this book are meant to be an essay in christology; but it is not possible to write on Jesus of Nazareth without touching on christology. All I wish to state is my belief that *opposition* between "christology from below" and "christology from above" is neither helpful nor sensible. What I mean by the terminology is whether one starts with Jesus of Nazareth or starts with the Johannine Logos who, in Jesus, became one of us. It is recognized that, while there is notable difference, there is no conflict between, let us say, the synoptists and John — or at least not when both are properly understood. The christology of Mark is a sophisticated christology, yet Mark — and the same is true of Luke and Matthew — knows nothing of pre-existence and incarnation. What I am saying is that faith and theology are not the same thing. Mark and John share the same faith — but their theology is spectacularly different. I have instanced Mark and John as representatives of New Testament christological views because it surely has to be that the New Testament has absolute priority as a *source* of christology. But, having said that, I go on to say that if there need be no conflict between christology from below and christology from above, the starting-point has to be from below — if only because there we find the historical starting-point.

Chalcedon

The fact remains that for centuries it has been assumed that the fifth-century Council of Chalcedon (451) had spoken the definitive christological word — all that remained was commentary. Christology became, in practice, an ever more subtle refinement of the language of Chalcedon. What we need to face, in this twentieth century, is that the philosophical thought-world (Middle Platonic) and Greek terminology of Chalcedon are foreign to us. Our English terms, nature, substance, person (these are the terms used in traditional christology) do not at all mean what the corresponding Greek terms *physis, ousia, hypostasis,* meant for fourth-fifth century Greeks. The argument that the Councils of Nicaea (325) and Chalcedon asserted that Jesus Christ is "of one substance with the Father" or that in him there are "two natures and one person" is invalid — simply because the words "substance," "nature," and "person" are English words with meanings quite different from the terms they are supposed to translate.

The situation is aggravated by the fact that it is not Chalcedon, but a certain interpretation of it, that has dominated medieval and later christology. Thus *an-hypostasia,* a denial that Jesus is a human person, goes quite beyond anything in Chalcedon. The fact is that the later interpretation of Chalcedon has become an albatross. Ironically,while the concern of Council was a defence of the true humanness of Jesus, the effect of the retention of its language of person and nature has been to turn Jesus into an alien among us.

In order properly to understand Chalcedon, one must look

to New Testament christology. Chalcedon cannot be in contradiction with the New Testament but it certainly does not reflect the whole of New Testament christology. On the other hand, modern christology, if it is to be authentic, cannot contradict the Chalcedonian statement. But it must be, at very least, a reinterpretation of it. Otherwise one would have to maintain that a fifth-century Council had spoken the last significant christological word. And that, in my book, is nonsense. Even apart from all that: how could a fifth-century declaration be a starting-point? The starting point of christology has to be its historical starting point: the New Testament. What marks christology today is a return to New Testament categories — and a translation of them into the language of our day.[6]

As an example of what I have in mind, I find the following statement wholly congenial:

> By his words and his praxis, Jesus himself changed the content of the word "God." If we do not allow him to change our image of God, we will not be able to say that *he* is our Lord and our God. To choose him as our God is to make him the source of our information about divinity and to refuse to superimpose upon him our own ideas of divinity.
>
> This is the meaning of the traditional assertion that Jesus is the Word of God. Jesus reveals God to us, God does not reveal Jesus to us. God is not the Word of Jesus, that is to say, our ideas about God cannot throw any light upon the life of Jesus. To argue from God to Jesus instead of arguing from Jesus to

---

[6]Wilfrid Harrington, "The Man Christ Jesus," (*Milltown Studies* No. 14, 1984, 2-3).

God is to put the cart before the horse. This, of course, is what many Christians have tried to do. It has generally led them into a series of meaningless speculations which only cloud the issue and which prevent Jesus from revealing God to us.[7]

Conclusion

While, as I have said, it is not my intent to get involved in christological questions, it was not out of place briefly to indicate some problems of later christology, if only because that may serve to underline the need for going back to the beginning, and be a salutary reminder that the real live person, Jesus of Nazareth, stands behind all christological speculation. I may effect my escape from a hasty venture into christology in order to bring this chapter and this first part of the book to a close. In six previous chapters I had sought to indicate that Jesus of Nazareth, ever an enigmatic figure, was always a controversial figure. It seems to me that, in christian tradition, there has been a firm tendency to downplay the humanness of this Son of man. I have noted the tendency in Matthew and Luke. I have suggested that the high Johannine christology was much influenced by historical circumstances. It might have been thought that nothing could be more in step with a faith proclamation, "the Word was made flesh,"

---

[7]Albert Nolan, *Jesus Before Christianity,* pp. 136-137. Albert Nolan, former Provincial of the Dominican Order in Southern Africa, was elected Master of the Dominican Order in September 1983. He declined the office on the plea that he wanted to continue his fight on behalf of the oppressed people of his native South Africa. His Dominican brethren, to their credit, appreciated his viewpoint and accepted his resignation.

than a wholly human Jesus. Yet, the Johannine Christ is not recognizably "one who in every respect has been tempted as we are" (Heb 4:15). Why? In good part because of sharp controversy within the Johannine community. A confrontational setting is not a really healthy setting for good theology. There is the risk of over-statement.

Have Christians even begun to learn that Jesus was not a man of confrontation? He challenged; but he would dialogue with anybody and would condemn nobody. He could not win, of course — and he did not. His failure, Paul would assure us, is the only victory.

II

———————————

PAUL

8

I MYSELF AM AN ISRAELITE

The first Christians confessed Jesus as Messiah. For Saul of Tarsus this was intolerable. That man, Jesus of Nazareth, had been rightly condemned by the sanhedrin and had been crucified. The curse of God had fallen upon him: "Cursed be everyone who hangs on a tree" (Dt 21:23; cf Gal 3:13). It was perverse and sinful to claim that Jesus was Messiah of Israel. Moreover, Paul perceived that the claim was a radical challenge to the Torah[1] and, therefore, to the heart of Judaism. For, if one upon whom Torah pronounced a curse was, at the same time, one acclaimed by God, then Torah had been set aside, and God was making a new declaration through Jesus — was, in fact, proclaiming a new Torah. No wonder, then, that Paul "persecuted the church of God violently and tried to destroy it" (Gal 2:13).

[1]For a pharisaic Jew the Torah (including the written Torah [the Pentateuch] and the oral law, the *Halakah*, the "tradition of the elders," Mk 7:3) expressed the fulness of the divine mind. In this situation the Torah took on an absolute value and one could concern oneself exclusively with the Law.

In dealing with Paul one has to realize that one is faced with a character of sheer integrity. Saul the Pharisee was perceptively aware of the threat posed by the Christian movement to his understanding of Judaism. He reacted with typical honesty and ardor. His subsequent bitter opposition to judaizers must have been baffling to them: he was rejecting the kind of person he had been. They acknowledged Jesus as Messiah but clung firmly to the saving role of Torah: "Unless you are circumcised according to the custom of Moses, you cannot be saved...It is necessary...to keep the law of Moses" (Acts 15:1, 5). Because they lacked his perception, they could not comprehend his "betrayal." They had come to terms, in their manner, with a crucified Messiah. For them the threat to Torah was the unqualified acceptance of Gentiles into the christian movement, for that implied that Torah was no longer the sole means of salvation. And Paul was chief architect of a gentile-christian movement.

If the judaizers were upset, what were Paul's former pharisaic colleagues to make of one who had gone over to the "enemy"? I believe it is abundantly clear that the break was extremely painful for Paul. He knew that, through his faith in Jesus Christ, he had come to fulfillment as a Jew. He found it hard to accept that most of his fellow Jews viewed the matter so differently. He never had any doubt about his own identity: "I myself am an Israelite" (Rom 11:1).

The Olive Tree

I find one of the most attractive traits of Paul to be his patriotism. He is a Jew and never, for a moment, would he contemplate any betrayal of his Jewishness. He had come to believe, with passionate conviction, that in Jesus he had found the Messiah, the goal of Jewish expectation. One may well find that chapters 9-11 of Romans do not represent the easiest and clearest part of Paul's writings. But one cannot fail to be moved by the passion behind these chapters. Paul simply will *not* accept that God has rejected his people (11:1). He is quite clear as to the privilege of his people: "They are Israelites, and to them belong the sonship, the glory, the covenants, the giving of the law, the worship, and the promises; to them belong the patriarchs, and of their race, according to the flesh, is the Christ" (9:4-5). His argumentation is tortuous, simply because the problem he addresses is so puzzling: how could God's people have failed to recognize God's Messenger?

He argues, almost despairingly, that not all Israelites are truly Israelites. "For not all who are descended from Israel (Jacob) belong to Israel, and not all are children of Abraham because they are his descendants; but 'Through Isaac shall your descendants be named.' This means that it is not the children of the flesh who are the children of God, but the children of the promise are reckoned as descendants" (9:6-8). This means that, however numerous the people of Israel, "only a remnant of them will be saved" (9:27). Next he turns to the stage prop of God the Potter (9:19-24). He hits rock bottom when he tries to convince us that the response of Gentiles to Christ will make Jews jealous and open their eyes (11:11-12). From there, though, it is all progress. He sternly warns Gentile Christians not to cherish any feelings of superiority. They must never forget that they are the wild olive branches grafted, gratuitously, on the chosen stock of the true olive, Israel (11:17-21).

Paul has never lost sight of his conviction that "the gifts and the call of God are irrevocable" (11:29). He had, quite openly, expressed his human doubts in face of a humanly incomprehensible situation. At the end, he puts his trust in God and he can declare, in words that have nothing to do with the logic of his argument up to now: "and so all Israel will be saved" (11:26). Indeed, Paul is going to take a giant step: "For God has consigned all men to disobedience, that he may have mercy upon all" (11:32). His declaration has to be seen in contrast to the unrelieved picture he has painted in Romans 1-3. But, then, that backdrop was meant to highlight the incredibly gracious saving gift of God. Paul had realized, what Jesus had found, that humankind does not want to acknowledge the foolish love of God.

To Him Be Glory

The hymn of Romans 11:33-36 undergirds Paul's optimistic conclusion. In 11:25 he had referred to the "mystery": the divine purpose that involved the salvation of "all Israel." He speaks, now, with charismatic conviction. The "mystery" has been revealed to him. The prevalent New Testament position is that the old Israel has been replaced by a new Israel. This view finds its most unsavory expression in statements of the "letters to the seven churches" of Revelation. It is found in the message to Smyrna: "I know your tribulation and your poverty...and the slander of those who say that they are Jews and are not, but are a synagogue of Satan" (Rev 2:9), and in the message to Philadelphia: "Behold, I will make those of the synagogue of Satan who say that they are Jews and are not, but lie . . ." (3:9). The arrogance is breathtaking. Two little christian communities look across at the corresponding Jewish ghettoes and declare: You Jews are liars; you have no right to call yourself Jews; we (Gentile Christians) are the *real* Jews! Surely Paul's conviction that "the gifts and the call of God are irrevocable" (Rom 11:29) must be preferred. And, surely, the basic ecumenism is not between the splintered parts of Christianity but between Judaism and Christianity. The challenge of Paul to Christians stands: "Remember it is not you that support the root, but the root that supports you" (11:18). Perhaps a salutary lesson of the apostle of the Gentiles for the Gentiles is a reminder of the incalculable Gentile debt to Israel.

Servant of Christ

In 2 Corinthians Paul vehemently defends his apostleship against opponents of his: christian missionaries of Jewish origin. They, evidently, had stressed their Jewishness: they were Hebrews, Israelites, descendants of Abraham (11:21-22). Paul makes equal claims. But when it comes to their further assertion that they are "servants of Christ" (11:23), he launches into a spirited demonstration of the fact that he is something much more (11:23-29). Clearly, his role of "servant of Christ" has not at all entailed any shading of his status as Hebrew, Israelite and son of Abraham.

Perhaps most interesting is the passage Philippians 3:4-8. There Paul poignantly spells out the difference between his life as a Christian and his life as a Pharisee. He had, indeed, experienced a conversion — a radical change. But, to his eternal credit, he does not disparage his past, he makes no apologies. He had been granted a new vision. In the light of it the past appeared in different guise. But he was able to acknowledge the integrity of his former life. One appreciates how he could write of his former co-religionists: "I bear them witness that they have a zeal for God" — though, in view of his own experience, he must immediately add: "but it is not enlightened" (Rom 10:2). It is a matter of enlightenment — not a lack of goodwill.

> If any other man thinks he has reason for confidence in the flesh, I have more: circumcised on the eighth day, of the people of Israel, of the tribe of Benjamin, a Hebrew born of Hebrews; as to the law a Pharisee, as to zeal a persecutor of the church, as to righteousness under the law blameless (Phil 3:4-6).

There is no hiding the pride that shines through these words: Paul is *proud* to be a Jew. And he was not afflicted with false humility. He who could declare of himself in relation to his fellow apostles: "I worked harder than any of them" (1 Cor 15:10) can also declare of his pharisaic past: "as to righteousness under the law blameless." We are faced with a man of unshakable integrity.

The Sabbath Is Made for Man

A measure of Paul's integrity is his total refusal to apologize for his religious past. The continuation of his Philippian statement — "Whatever gain I had, I counted as loss for the sake of Christ" (Phil 3:7) — ought not be read as an apology. He is simply declaring that the gospel reverses the values of the world. That is quite clear from the following verse: "Indeed I count everything as loss because of the surpassing worth of knowing Christ Jesus my Lord" (3:8). The Paul whose perspicacity led him to identify the threat of the christian movement to his pharisaic zeal for the law is the same Paul who, following his encounter with Christ, became the Apostle.

> Paul can never be accused of indifference: the same missionary zeal by which he distinguished himself in his career as a Pharisee marks his life as a Christian. Converted, called, missioned, he now channels this zealous energy into spreading the gospel. But there is a difference; otherwise this would not be true conversion. Fidelity to the gospel requires that Paul's zeal be expressed in charity rather than strict adherence to law that could lead to the excesses of persecution. Not by force but by preaching, Paul seeks to win the obedience of faith. At a time when tension between Jews and Christians was mounting, Paul relinquished brutal weapons while aggressively and ambitiously following his call to preach the gospel to the ends of the earth. His zeal did not weaken but it transformed him from persecutor to victim. In his own life he fleshed out the consequences of learning that charity is more important than law, people more important than rules. There is here in Paul's own life a radical critique of "religion."[2]

[2]Mary Ann Getty, *Philippians and Philemon* (Wilmington, DE: M. Glazier, 1980, 52).

Salvation Is Gift

We shall see that Paul, the sometime model observer of Torah, ended by rejecting Torah. Not for a moment did he turn his back on Israel. There clearly was no love lost between him and judaizers — converts from pharisaic Judaism who maintained the necessity of observance of Torah even for Gentile Christians. How deep his antipathy went is nowhere better expressed than in Philippians 3:2 — "Look out for the dogs...those who mutilate the flesh." "Dogs" was the derogatory term used by Jews of Gentiles. Here Paul applies it to Jews (the judaizers were Jewish Christians). He wants to hurt — and he knows how to hurt! Again, his rejection of judaizers is in no way a rejection of Israel.

To Paul the tragedy of Israel is clear — a perception that came out of his own pharisaic past. While acknowledging that his people had a zeal for God he admitted that it was not enlightened. And the reason is that "being ignorant of the righteousness that comes from God, and seeking to establish their own, they did not submit to God's righteousness" (Rom 10:3). He pushes to its logical conclusion the way of fidelity to Torah: the faithful observer of Torah effectively wins his own salvation. If the way of standing right with God is the way of meticulous observance, then the faithful observer has earned salvation. Paul had come to understand that salvation is gift — a gift to be received. Torah is not the way to salvation. "For Christ is the end of the law, that every one who has faith may be justified" (Rom 10:4).

9

THE POWER OF GOD FOR SALVATION

Saul, Saul, why do you persecute me? Who are you, Lord? I am Jesus whom you are persecuting.

(Acts 9:4-5; 22:7-8; 26:14-15).

Luke has three times related Paul's Damascus experience. Because Paul is so important to him in his account of Christian origins it is not surprising that he has emphasized so the "conversion" of his hero. Paul himself refers to the episode more circumspectly:

When he who had set me apart before I was born, and had called me through his grace, was pleased to reveal his Son to me, in order that I might preach him among the Gentiles...

(Gal 1:15-16).

Just before that statement Paul had declared: "I advanced in Judaism beyond many of my own age among my people, so extremely zealous was I for the traditions of my fathers" (1:14). One must be very careful in speaking of the "conversion" of Paul. It is certainly wrong to think of it in terms of crossing from one religion to another — the movement which Paul now joined did not become a religion wholly distinct from Judaism until after Paul's death. We must think of his "conversion" in terms of *metanoia* — a radical change of attitude. What happened was that he came to look upon Judaism in a fresh light. His new conviction that Jesus of Nazareth was indeed the Messiah of Israel's expectation, and that Jesus had brought another understanding of God, changed his outlook and his whole life. The pharisaic way of standing right with God could never again be his way. Henceforth he will see God through the eyes of the Son. For, though he was to write of God revealing his Son to him he had, in fact, realized that the Son had revealed his God to him.

Paul's Damascus experience, however radical, was still a profoundly human experience. A *radical* change could not happen overnight. Paul had to assimilate the experience, had to think things over. He speaks vaguely of a sojourn in Arabia and a return to Damascus (Gal 1:17); it is significant that three years were to elapse before his visit to Jerusalem. We have observed that he never made excuses for his past. What had happened was that his encounter with the risen Jesus forced him to re-evaluate his whole religious outlook. And this led him, inevitably, to another understanding of God. And led him to the distinctive features of his "gospel": salvation for Jew *and* Gentile, and justification by faith.

There Is neither Jew nor Greek

The gospels show Jesus as one who acknowledged and respected the traditional Jewish distinction between Jew and

Gentile. It is enough to recall the Matthean saying: "I was sent only to the lost sheep of the house of Israel" (Mt 15:24) and his words to the Syrophoenician woman — "it is not right to take the children's bread and throw it to the dogs" (Mk 7:27). Before long, Christians came to discern the universal drift in Jesus' message. This is emphatically expressed in the conclusion of Matthew's gospel, in the commission of the risen Lord: "Go therefore and make disciples of all nations..." (Mt 28:19) — the assured conviction of a church that had reached out in a mission to the Gentiles. Acts of the Apostles attests that Paul played a dominant role in that vital turn. Let it be said, though, that Luke does not claim that Paul was the first missionary to the Gentiles, nor the only one. He admits that some of those who were "scattered because of the persecution that arose over Stephen...men of Cyprus and Cyrene, on coming to Antioch spoke to the Greeks also, preaching the Lord Jesus" (Acts 11:19-20). Still, the major role he subsequently attributes to Paul is borne out by Paul himself in Galatians, chapter 2 — for that matter, throughout Paul's writings. Nowhere better than in Romans does he spell out his deepest conviction that God is, indeed, God of Jew and Gentile. That point is made, without more ado, in the theme of the epistle (1:16-17):

> For I am not ashamed of the gospel: it is the power of God for salvation to everyone who has faith, to the Jew first and also to the Greek. For in it the righteousness of God is revealed through faith for faith.

The Power of God

It is immediately clear that, for Paul, the "gospel" is the "power of God"; it is not a philosophy nor a religious system — nor even a message. It is power; but "power," in Paul's paradoxical view, is nothing other the "word of the cross" (1 Cor 1:18). That power is responsive to *faith*: the acknowledgment of the power of God at work in the life, death and resurrection of Jesus Christ; the trusting of oneself to that God; the submission of oneself to his saving power; the realization that one has no claims on God; the giving of oneself, and gladly, over to his gracious power.

"To the Jew first and also to the Greek": Paul is not thinking only of the historical fact that the Jews were the first to hear the gospel. There is much more to it than that. Though he is insistent that the gospel is "for the Gentiles too" he is adamant in his assertion of the election of Israel. It cannot be that Israel had been set aside to make place for a new "Israel." *The* people of God has to include Jew and Gentile.

"For in it the righteousness of God is revealed." The current translations — "righteousness" or "justice" — of the word *diakaiosyne* are not adequate; worse than that, they are misleading. The fact remains that we are stuck with them; but we can at least be alert to their shortcomings. The "righteousness of God" is regularly taken to be a divine attribute. Paul thinks of an act or activity of God. And when he says that "the righteousness of God is revealed" he means that God's activity is manifest in the field of human experience. This becomes clear when we look at the background which for Paul is of course, the Old

Testament. Behind the word *dikaiosynē* in the Septuagint (the pre-Christian Greek translation of the Hebrew Scriptures) is the Hebrew *sedaqa*. The root verb *sadaq* means "to put in the right," and also "to vindicate" a person who has been victimized. A judge is not a just judge by upholding an abstract legal standard, but because he vindicates the cause of the oppressed — he is champion of "the widow and orphan." His "righteousness" is seen in the "justification" of those who are victims of oppression.

Already this glance at the biblical background to *dikaiosynē* suggests that to think of it in terms of *justice* can be quite misleading. Our traditional symbol of justice — the blindfolded lady with the scales — has little to do with biblical justice, has nothing to do with God's justice. The simple fact is that God, by our standards, is quite *unjust*. I regularly try out on my students and listeners the statement: "God is a just God who deals with us fairly." At first I get approving nods until I challenge them really to look at the declaration. Then I get sheepish smiles. Which of us wants a *just* God? I certainly do not want a just God who might deal with me fairly — I want a loving God who will deal with me mercifully! Well it is for us that our God is unjust. We find our hope in the injustice of our God.

While it is true that Paul's "justification" has something of a forensic tone, a smack of the law-court, his use of the term is paradoxical. That is clear when, in Romans 5:6-11, he describes the manner of justification: "While we were yet helpless, at the right time, Christ died for the ungodly" (v. 6). If God be Judge, he is the Judge who acquits the guilty. It is not a question of handing down a suspended sentence or a lenient sentence. No, he simply accepts the plea of "guilty" — and dismisses the case! Such conduct is an affront to our idea of justice. But God is doing it all the time. We should rejoice in the injustice of our God. *We* have a problem in our striving to reconcile God's mercy with his justice. Let us not lose sleep over it! *God* has no such problem.

Justified by his Grace

> But now the righteousness of God has been manifested apart from the law, although the law and the prophets bear witness to it, the righteousness of God through faith in Jesus Christ for all who believe. For there is no distinction; since all have sinned and fall short of the glory of God, they are justified by his grace as a gift, through the redemption which is in Christ Jesus, whom God put forward as an expiation by his blood, to be received by faith (Rom 3:21-25).

It is true that the term *dikaiosynē* carries, too, the connotation of an assertion of rights. What we should bear in mind is that it, or any term, when predicated of God, always means something quite different from its meaning in a merely human context. That is what Paul had in mind when he declared: "the foolishness of God is wiser than men" (1 Cor 1:25). Gods *dikaiosynē* is, indeed, his laying claim to us; it is an assertion of his rights. That assertion, however, is made not in a spirit of domination but wholly on our behalf. We had been slaves of the tyrants *Hamartia* (sin) and *Thanatos* (death). Now God declares: "You are mine." Where another lord might declare: "I am your lord: obey!", our God says to us: "I am your Father; you are my children. Come to me!" For our part, we must let it be; we must say our "yes" to God's claim on us. That is what *faith* is: saying yes to God; letting God be God *for us.* It is through Jesus Christ that God makes his claim. He is our God "who did not spare his own Son but gave him up for us all" (8:32). That, more than anything else, shows the character of God's "lordship," of his *dikaiosynē.*

For there is no distinction" (3:22): faith through Jesus Christ is now and henceforth the only path to salvation for Jew and Gentile alike. All humankind had "fallen short of the glory of God" (3:23), that is to say, were no longer truly in the image of God. When we acknowledge God's claim to us this image is restored. Because he lays claim to us as sinners we are justified "as a gift" (3:24). To "justify" means to pronounce just; because it is God who justifies we are truly made "just." By letting God be "just," by letting him be gracious in our regard, we are renewed, we are re-created. God's saving power — that is what "grace" means — brings about the new creation.

At this point (vv. 24-25) Paul introduces the terms "redemption," "expiation" and "blood" — terms that later theology was to understand in ways that regularly departed from Paul's usage, ways that, often enough, amounted to a travesty of his thought. In point of fact, the terms are not difficult to understand rightly — provided we appreciate the sense of the Hebrew and biblical ideas which formed the atmosphere of Paul's thinking.

Redemption

The word *apolytrōsis* commonly designated the price paid to free a slave or a prisoner of war. In Paul's vocabulary the term meant the act of redeeming. He used the word not in the contemporary Greek sense but in the light of Old Testament understanding. Thus, when the Israelites were liberated from bondage in Egypt they regarded themselves as slaves "redeemed" by Yahweh (Dt 7:8) and the later prophets similarly spoke of liberation from captivity in Babylon as "redemption" (Is 51:11). For Paul the word meant freedom, liberation. Our justification depends on the fact that God has intervened to liberate his people from bondage to sin.

Then there is the term *hilastērion*. In Greek writers the root-verb has two meanings: "to placate" a man or a god; "to expiate" a sin. In the Septuagint the first meaning is not used in reference to God while the other meaning is frequent. There can be no doubt at all that for Paul the noun means "an act by which guilt is removed." He is declaring that Christ's death is the means by which God forgives sin. Finally, the word "blood" makes clear that Paul thinks of the death of Jesus in sacrificial terms: he laid down his life in self-dedication to God and on our behalf. And the divine act of redemption becomes effective "by faith" — the human response to God's gracious deed.

In my opinion the message of our passage has never been more neatly expressed than by C.H. Dodd.[1]

---

[1] *The Epistle of St. Paul to the Romans* (London: Collins, 1959, 80).

We find that Paul is combining three metaphors: the first taken from the lawcourt — the metaphor of justification; the second taken from the institution of slavery — that of emancipation; the third taken from the sacrificial ritual of ancient religion — that of expiation by blood. Under all three metaphors he describes an act of God for men. In the first, God takes the part of the judge who acquits the prisoner; in the second, that of the benefactor who secures freedom for the slave; in the third, that of the priest who makes expiation. But in Paul's biblical background all these metaphors had already moved part of the way into reality. The deliverance of Israel from bondage had been described by the prophets both as "justification" and as "emancipation"; and the language of the Septuagint shows that there was the forgiveness granted by God himself . . . (Paul is concerned with the status of men and women before God) which is altered by an act of God himself — from condemnation to acquittal, from bondage to freedom, from guilt to innocence. The change of status described in this threefold way is, as he presently shows, accompanied by an inward change from sinfulness to right living, from moral impotence to moral competence. But what he is here concerned to make clear is that by no possible effort of his own could man alter his status before God, any more than a guilty prisoner could acquit himself, or a slave free himself, or an "unclean" person become "clean" without supernatural means; but that God, by a sheer act of grace, has made this change of status possible.

If God Is for Us

Paul had spent most of the first three chapters of Romans painting in the starkest colors the helpless plight of humankind before the coming of Christ. It is the backdrop of his picture of God's incredible love towards sinful humankind. "God shows his love for us in that while we were yet sinners Christ died for us" (5:8) — for us "the ungodly" (v. 6), the estranged from God. Paul goes on to describe the deed of God as reconciliation: "we are reconciled . . .we have received our reconciliation" (5:10-11). We have noted above that *hilastērion,* in Paul's usage, cannot possibly mean the placating of an angry God. If there were any doubt, it must be laid now. It could not be clearer that it is not God who is the one reconciled. We are reconciled to God: it is *he* who does the reconciling. "God was in Christ, reconciling the world to himself" (2 Cor 5:19). One wonders how theories of satisfaction and propitiation could ever have been constructed and, more disturbingly, how they have prevailed.[2]

---

[2]Because this matter is so important it may be helpful to list some key texts which underline the sheer perversity of the accepted "satisfaction theory." "If while we were enemies we were reconciled to God by the death of his Son, much more, now that we are reconciled, shall we be saved by his life" (Rom 5:10). "He who did not spare his own Son but gave him up for us all, will he not also give us all things with him" (Rom 8:32).

"For God so loved the world that he gave his only Son, that whoever believes in him should not perish but have eternal life. For God sent the Son into the world, not to condemn the world, but that the world might be saved through him" (Jn 3:16-17).

"God is love. In this the love of God was made manifest among us, that God sent his only Son into the world, so that we might live through him. In this is love, not that we loved God but that he loved us and sent his Son to be the expiation for our sins" (1 Jn 4:8-9).

That same purpose of God is implicitly present in the high priest christology of Hebrews (2:17-18; 4:14-16; 5:7-10; 7:25). The truth is: theories of propitiation and satisfaction can stand only if such texts are overlooked — indeed only if the whole New Testament is ignored.

A Feudal Lord?

Christ died *for us*. It is not surprising that theology should have concerned itself with explanations of the significance of Jesus' death. One way was to take "for us" as meaning *substitution*: Jesus had suffered instead of us — and that is surely not what Paul meant. The most influential attempt at explanation has turned out to be the Satisfaction Theory propounded by Anselm of Canterbury (died 1109). Cultural setting is always important and Anselm's cultural background was the world of feudalism. A jealously guarded value of that world was the right to one's honor. A feudal lord could not ignore or overlook a personal insult. In face of affront, only two courses lay open to him: to punish, or to accept adequate reparation. Anselm applied this principle to God. God had been grossly offended by human sin; he must have reparation; otherwise he must punish. The snag is that sinful humankind is incapable of making adequate restitution for the injury inflicted. But the Son of God could and did offer satisfaction, by means of his death. God accepted his reparation and forgave us.

Given his presupposition, Anselm's theory had about it an impressive logic and clarity. But that presupposition carried a fatal flaw: God is *not* a feudal lord! What is upsetting is that the theory had gone practically unchallenged almost up to the present. Indeed, one believes it would still be the accepted view of many Christians. This fact is all the more disturbing because the theory is a travesty of the gospel. God is not a sulking God, jealous of his honor, a God who "graciously" forgive provided he gets his pound of flesh. That "God" is surely not the Father of our Lord Jesus Christ.

Besides, the theory has got the whole matter upside down. "Anselm's theory in all its forms makes God the *object* of reconciliation and is thus very far from the fundamental assertion of Paul: 'God was in Christ, reconciling the world to himself' (2 Cor 5:19). For Paul God is the *subject* of reconciliation, the one who *does* it."[3]

The Love of God in Christ Jesus

In the conclusion of this chapter it will suffice to look to Paul's moving peroration in chapter eight of Romans (8:31-39). That remarkable declaration of his certainty of salvation is a summary of the whole first part of Romans and of Paul's gospel in general. It tells us that God's love is *like this*. It assures us that here is the God who has laid claim to us and has given us a claim on him.

> [31]What then shall we say to this? If God is for us, who is against us? [32]He who did not spare his own Son but gave him up for us all, will he not also give us all things with him? [33]Who will bring any charge against God's elect? It is God who justifies! [34]Who is to condemn? Christ Jesus who died, yes, who was raised from the dead, who is at the right hand of God, who indeed intercedes for us! [35]Who shall separate us

[3]John C. Dwyer, *Son of God and Son of Man*, 163. His observation is sadly true: "The view of God implied by this theory has been propagated in countless sermons and manuals of piety and devotion. Time and again we have heard variations on this theme: God is the one who must be propitiated or appeased and we must make atonement to him for our sins. He is pictured as one who is ready to strike unless the appropriate peace-offering is made and who is prevented from exacting a terrible vengeance only by the fact that his Son Jesus Christ 'gets in the way' and absorbs the divine wrath which was directed towards us" (162).

from the love of Christ? Shall tribulation, or distress, or persecution, or famine, or nakedness, or peril, or sword? [36]As it is written.

For thy sake we are being killed all the day long;
We are regarded as sheep to be slaughtered.

[37]No, in all these things we are more than conquerors through him who loved us. [38]For I am sure that neither death, nor life, nor angels, nor principalities, nor things present, nor things to come, nor powers, [39]nor height, nor depth, nor anything else in all creation, will be able to separate us from the love of God in Christ Jesus our Lord.

We learn at once who God is: he is *God for us.* It is as good a definition of God as we might hope for. He is the loving God who created us and has called us to be his daughters and his sons. The question of v. 32 can have one answer only. The giving of his Son shows, beyond doubt, that God is in deadly earnest. Father and Son were prepared to go to any length to save man from himself. God gave his Son without any precondition; he took the risk. The death of the Son was, at the deepest level, a sacrifice made by God.

A problem with verses 33-34 is how they are to be punctuated.[4] The choice made here is that of two questions with ironical answers. Who can bring a charge? God —who justifies! It is really another way of putting the question of v. 31 — "If God is for us, who is against us?" Can we imagine that the God who, in our helplessness, has, at such a cost, taken his saving initiative, is now going to be our Judge? And who will condemn us? Christ Jesus, who died for us, who

---

[4]The manuscripts are no help since they are devoid of any punctuation.

intercedes for us![5] Again it is another way of putting a question, this time the following question: "Who shall separate us from the love of Christ?" Christ's love for us is dramatically present in his sacrificial death and in his efficacious intercession. Tribulations and distress cannot separate us from that love of Christ. It is evident that the suffering in question is especially suffering that comes in the service of the gospel. It follows, though, that no trials of our human lot can come between the Christian and that unyielding love. With the Jewish and Greek worlds of his day in mind, Paul insists, for those who believed that angelic beings had influence over humans, and for others who believed in astrology,[6] that none of these "forces" had any effect on God's love for us. The simple fact that nothing in the whole creation — which is *God's* creation —can come between us and God's love for us, concretely expressed in the unqualified giving of his Son for our sake. It has been finely said: "There is no arguing with such a certainty. Either you simply don't believe it or you recognize

[5]It is remarkable how firmly the New Testament presents Christ as intercessor or advocate — and it is sad to reflect that tradition has regularly cast him as judge.

"He is able for all time to save those who draw near to God through him, since he always lives to make intercession for them" (Heb 7:25; cf 9:24).

"If any one does sin, we have an advocate (*paraklētos*) with the Father Jesus Christ the righteous" (1 Jn 2:1).

"Christ Jesus who died, yes, who was raised from the dead, who is at the right hand of God, who indeed intercedes for us" (Rom 8:34).

[6]"nor height, nor depth" — astrological terms referring to the highest and lowest point of stars above the horizon.

it as the word of God."[7] Let us hear Paul's words again—this in striking paraphrase.[8]

Romans 8:31-39

What can we possibly add to what we have already said? God is caring for us, who or what can *possibly* harm us?

Since God did not withhold from us the most precious of all gifts, even the life of His own Son to give Life to us all, can we not be certain that He would not *possibly* refuse us whatever else we may need?

When God has chosen us to be His special friends, can anyone's misunderstanding or even rejection *possibly* have any hold on us? Who can bring any real charge against us? Certainly *not* the God who pardons us from all charges! Who can ever really condemn us? Certainly *not* the merciful Christ Jesus!

Why, not only did He actually die for us. He also rose from death to abide in the presence of God Himself, where He prays unceasingly on our behalf.

Thus, nothing whatsoever can take us away from the love of Jesus. Even if we are anxious, distressed, or attacked, even if we are without food and clothing, even if we are being threatened or even assaulted, still nothing can ever take us away from Him.

After all, the psalm says: "For Your sake, O Lord, we die each day and are counted as sheep for the slaughter." And

[7]C.H. Dodd, *op. cit.*, 160.

[8]Paraphrase by Penny Livermore.

such trials as these are sent to us only so that, in the end, we may overcome them — overcome them through the strength of His love.

So, I repeat that I am *absolutely sure* of this: No experience whatsoever in dying or living, nothing in the realm of ideas or spirits, nothing in the realm of earthbound reality, nothing in the future, nor any kind of power, nothing concerning the stars of heaven or creatures of earth, can ever — ever — possibly take us away from God's love shining forth upon us in Jesus.

10

FOR FREEDOM

There is no doubt that when he wrote Galatians, Paul was an angry man. That fact is clear from the very style of the letter. He departs from his otherwise invariable custom of a "thankgiving" after the initial address and, instead, breaks into a pained: "I am astonished . . ." (Gal 1:6). The judaizers who are, successfully it appears, persuading the Galatians to take on observance of the Mosaic law evoke memories, that still rankle, of former opponents of his in Antioch — those "false brethren secretly brought in, who slipped in to spy out our freedom which we have in Christ Jesus, that they might bring us into bondage" (2:4). Luke, I believe, has provided the key to Paul's impassioned reaction. In Luke's account of that Antioch situation (Acts 15:11), the Pauline opponents, described as "believers who belonged to the party of the Pharisees" (15:5) and natives of Judea, had gone to Antioch to confront Gentile Christians: "Unless you are circumcised according to the custom of Moses, you cannot be saved" (15:1). Both Acts 15 and Galatians 2 agree that Paul's view won the day: one could be Christian without becoming a Jew. The "pharisee party" had suffered a resounding defeat. But this upset did not signal the end of them. Paul had to sustain their assaults throughout his ministry. It is not irrelevant to observe that while the judaizers are, today, figures of vague historical interest, Paul continues to be a vital force.

Christ, the End of the Law.

Paul's own attitude to Torah was radical. Nowhere is this more evident than in Galatians 3:23-26. There he calls the Torah a *paidagōgos* — "the law was our custodian until Christ came...but now that faith has come we are no longer under a custodian" (3:24-25). In Greco-Roman society the *paidagōgos* (here rendered "custodian") was the slave-tutor of his master's son, one responsible for his education. He had great, but temporary, authority. As Paul puts it, that child, though he be heir (and future master) is "under guardians and trustees until the date set by the father" (4:2). That date marks the end of the role and authority of the *paidagōgos*. The analogy is clear: with the coming of Christ and the inauguration of his new age, the Torah has had its day. Not only is Torah not a necessary means of salvation (the judaizer contention) it has nothing to say to the Christian.

There is close relationship between Galatians and Romans, but it is noticeable that the tone of Romans is the more circumspect. For one thing, in Romans, Paul is addressing a community he had not yet visited (whereas the Galatian community was of his own founding). Besides, he is evidently anxious to ingratiate himself with the Roman Christians. Though the make-up of the Roman community has been variously assessed (predominantly Jewish? or Gentile?) the letter may be fairly characterized as a dialogue with Judaism.[1] It is noteworthy, then, that while Paul avoids the metaphor of *paidagōgos* — which would have been offensive to Jew or judaizer — he sticks to his guns and maintains the end of Torah. This surely follows from the statement: "Now the righteousness of God had been manifested apart from law" (Rom 3:21a). For that matter, the further comment: "although the law and the prophets bear witness to it" (v. 21b) is a close parallel to Galatians 3:23-25. And when Paul declares that "Christ is the end of the law" (10:4) his meaning is quite clear from the immediate context (9:31-33; 10:5-13) — a meaning reinforced by passages such as 3:21; 5:20; 7:1-25; 8:2-3, not to mention the theology of Galatians. The question is not the fact of Paul's stance *vis-à-vis* the Torah but, rather, why he took and maintained that stance. To answer the question one must look to Paul's first assessment of the christian movement and his reassessment of it in the light of his Damascus experience.

For Saul of Tarsus the claim of "the Nazoreans" that the crucified Jesus of Nazareth was God's Messiah was perverse and sinful — how could one accursed be the Messiah?[2] Their further claim that God had raised him from the dead, implying God's approval of Jesus, was a challenge to the authority of Torah. But when the moment came for God "to reveal his Son" to Saul (Gal 1:16) all began to appear in a

---

[1]J. Christiann Beker, *Paul the Apostle* (Philadelphia: Fortress, 1980, 74-83).

[2]See p. 111.

wholly new light. He had been brought to see that God's definitive grace is embodied in the promise to Abraham which reaches beyond Israel to all the nations of the earth (cf Gen 12:3; Gal 3:14). The author of Ephesians correctly caught his drift. Jesus Christ has "broken down the dividing wall of hostility" (Eph 2:12) — the wall of Torah which had separated Jew and Gentile.

For all his new vision there remained, in Paul, a tension between his being in Christ and his being a Jew. But he would not resolve that tension by collapsing Jew and Gentile into a third entity. And it is this which explains a certain ambivalence in his attitude to the law, a seeming contradiction between such strong statements we have been noting and others that sound differently.[3] The church is the "Israel of God" (Gal 6:16) — a community in which Jewish Christians might retain their attachment to Torah and Temple and in which Gentile Christians might make their way without Torah or Temple. In the "church of God" Paul looked for freedom, not uniformity. His harsh attitude to "law" — in Galatians, for instance — was, in part at least, because legalism brings a stultifying sameness, because it stifles the Spirit. And Christ has called us to freedom, the freedom of the children of God (Gal 5:1; Rom 8:21).

---

[3]E.g. "But now the righteousness of God has been manifested apart from law, although the law and the prophets bear witness to it" (Rom 3:21); "So the law is holy, and the commandment is holy, and just and good" (7:12); "to those under the law I became as one under the law . . . that I might win those under the law (1 Cor 9:20).

Not All Things Build Up

"For freedom Christ has set us free" (Gal 5:1). The tautology is firmly deliberate. Paul really believed in freedom, believed in it as an essential value of genuinely christian life — because what he so thoroughly believed in and inculcated was *christian* freedom. It seems to me that an especially precious legacy of Paul is his understanding of freedom. It is a treasure that his heirs have too rarely recognized or appreciated. This fact will, I believe, be readily discernible once we have outlined the distinctive features of Paul's sophisticated concept of freedom. And, for that, it is enough to look to Galatians and First Corinthians.

It is evident from Paul's extant letters to Corinth (he wrote at least two other letters besides our 1, 2 Corinthians (1 Cor 5:9; 2 Cor 2:3- 4, 9) that the Corinthian community was turbulent. "For it has been reported to me by Chloe's people that there is quarelling among you, my brethren. What I mean is that each one of you says, 'I belong to Paul,' or 'I belong to Apollos,' or 'I belong to Cephas' or 'I belong to Christ'" (1 Cor 1:11-12). Just here is the exasperating feature of the letter. There is no doubt that the Corinthians are fully aware of the situation to which Paul refers. *We* are left to guess at the cause of the malaise. But, whatever may have been the reason or reasons, the reality of serious dissension is manifest.

The Corinthian community was markedly charismatic —chapters 12-14 offer abundant evidence of that. Some, perhaps most, believed that they were Spirit-seized people; hence their slogan: "All things are lawful for me." What Paul does, and tellingly, is to take their vaunted slogan and add his own rider:

> "All things are lawful for me" — but not all things are helpful
> "All things are lawful for me" — but I will not be enslaved by anything (6:12)
> "All things are lawful" — but not all things are helpful
> "All things are lawful" — but not all things build up (10:23).

Only what is "helpful" or "builds up" is consistent with true freedom, a freedom whose exercise is designed to reinforce the bonds that bind humans together in Christ. This freedom is circumscribed by "love which binds things together in perfect harmony" (Col 3:14). In Christ one is freed for love, and love is real only in service. In specifying "service" it would be unwise to overlook the thoroughly christian statement of a blind Milton: "They also serve, who only stand and wait."

The Strong and the Weak

One of the questions exercising Corinthian Christians was that of "food offered to idols" (8:1). In the pagan society of the day the frequent feasts and ceremonies regularly involved animal sacrifices. A proportion of the sacrificial meat went to the priests who commonly sold the surplus in the open market. Besides, recurring events like marriages and funerals involved meals in a pagan religious setting — meals at which idol-meats were served. All of this raised a series of problems for Christians. Might one take part in a sacred meal? Might one buy meat that had been offered to idols?

Might one eat such meat at a meal to which one had been invited? It appears that many at Corinth, taking their stand on monotheism and arguing that an idol had no real existence, maintained that the meats in question were clean; these are "the strong." It is easy to guess that those who took this view were Jewish Christians. Their native contempt of idolatry would enable them to adopt a cavalier attitude towards this whole matter of pagan meals and idol-meats. For Gentile Christians, in this respect "the weak," it was a different matter altogether. They had come from that pagan background. As they would see it, they had *escaped* from that environment. Participation in a ritual meal would seem to embroil them again.

Let us visualize a situation that is not far-fetched. A Gentile Christian was invited to the wedding of a relative; an invitation was likewise extended to a Jewish Christian friend of the family. The latter accepted with alacrity; the former was in a quandary. This ex-pagan could end up, against his better judgment and with an uneasy conscience, eating idol-meats. It was the kind of situation Paul envisaged: "Some, through being hitherto accustomed to idols, eat food as really offered to an idol; and their conscience, being weak, is defiled . . . For if any one sees you, a man of knowledge, at table in an idol's temple, might he not be encouraged, if his conscience is weak, to eat food offered to idols?" (8:7, 10). The presence of a fellow (Jewish) Christian at a family wedding placed the Gentile Christian in a cruel dilemma: he had either to offend his family or act against his conscience.

In the language of the old-style moral theology handbook: *quid ad casum* (how is the situation to be handled)? Paul does not hesitate. In view of the dire consequence: "So by your knowledge this weak man is destroyed, the brother for whom Christ died" (8:11) his unequivocal judgment is: "if food is a cause of my brother's falling, I will never eat meat, lest I cause my brother to fall" (8:13). If this seems strong language, it is all the more remarkable that nowhere does Paul tell the Strong what to do. He firmly draws attention to aspects of the situation which they had overlooked. Whether or not this would affect their future conduct has to be their own decision. Paul will not be a surrogate conscience for them. Consistently, he will not present the Weak with an open check. He exorts them to inform their conscience (10:28-29); they have an obligation in charity to do so. With the interests of the Strong in mind he positively challenges the Weak: "Why should my liberty be determined by another man's scruples?" (10:29). For the one as for the other, loving concern is the only valid touchstone. Whether of the Strong or of the Weak, the brother or sister is always one "for whom Christ died." The whole matter boils down to one simple truth: christian freedom is ever circumscribed by love.

Christian Freedom

In 1 Corinthians 13 it is obvious that the positive aspects of *agapē* (love) had been suggested to Paul by the life and example of Jesus Christ. One needs only to substitute "Jesus" for "love" to see that. When all is put in terms of him then it is indeed true that love is patient and kind, rejoices in the right, bears all things, hopes all things, endures all things (1 Cor 13:4-7). It seems equally clear that Paul's grasp of freedom has been inspired by that same Jesus, that Son of man who came "not to be served but to serve, and to give his life as a ransom for many" (Mk 10:45). One uses the word "inspired" advisedly. Paul's concept of christian freedom is so obviously right. And that concept stands in sharp focus against Paul's concern in Galatians and 1 Corinthians with two contrasting enemies of freedom.

We have seen that when Paul learned that one of his churches, the Galatian community, was in danger of falling under the sway of judaizers and was looking for the false security of observance he reacted violently. An object lesson, unhappily almost wholly lost on Christians down the centuries, is the striking fact that the one time that Paul "pulls rank" — when he, in Galatians 1-2 spells out his apostolic authority and insists that it came directly "through Jesus Christ and God the Father" — he does so in the interest of *freedom*. He insists on his authority, not to browbeat the Galatians, not to awe them into submission, but in an almost desperate attempt to get them off their knees, to get them to accept the burden of responsibility and to take the risk of making decisions for themselves. They were welcoming the judaizers who offered them the security that came from clinging to Torah, thus freeing them from the responsibility of personal decision. Henceforth, their life would be mapped out for them: they had only to do or to avoid as the law prescribed. They were ready to shrug off responsibility and let an external moral directive carry the burden of decision.

There is another enemy of freedom: exaggeration. This Paul found in Corinth. He recognized that the attitude both of the charismatics and of "the strong" was based on a misunderstanding of christian freedom. The freedom that characterizes christian living is twofold — a freedom *from* and a freedom *to*. Within the christian community the Christian is, ideally, free from sin and free from law. However, to take this new freedom as freedom *to* do whatever one wishes, to push ahead regardless, is a grave error to which the Corinthians had succumbed. To absolutize freedom, to transfer to "freedom *to*" the absolute character of "freedom *from*," is to lose it, to become *enslaved*. Consideration for the needs of others is always the primary factor in the Christian's moral judgment; it must condition the exercise of his freedom.

Paul was unhappy with both Galatia and Corinth but he could relate more sympathetically to the Corinthian situation. The Galatians were seeking security. He saw clearly, what later christian communities were to learn to their cost, that this attitude made for immaturity and hampered love. It was a misunderstanding of the role of law. Law, in this view, can be the adequate expression of God's will and so one can limit oneself, in one's response to God, to what is prescribed in the law. And this brings a false sense of security because, having fulfilled the law, a person assumes that he or she stands right with God. There is something frightening in the realization that an attitude which eventually was to become prevalent enough in the church to be regarded as "normal," had not only been sharply criticized by Paul, but was the very attitude repudiated by Jesus himself!

Of Your Own Free Will

For Saul of Tarsus the prescriptions of Torah expressed the will of God and were normative in the strictest sense. For Paul, the precepts of Torah were guidelines to be followed with discretion in working out the Christian's response to the call of God in Christ. And one does not give unqualified obedience to guidelines. Directives which Paul issued were always in the practical area (e.g. 2 Thes 3:6, 10-11; 1 Cor 7:17; 11:34; 16:1). In strictly moral matters he refrained, absolutely, from laying down the law. His concern was with the authenticity of the action which must come from a decision as to what is the christian course of action. The freedom that is essential for such a responsible decision is destroyed by any form of compulsion — such as a binding precept.

Paul's view is very clearly expressed in *Philemon*. He tells Philemon, bluntly enough, what he *ought* to do, but he refuses to order him. "Though I am bold enough in Christ to command you to do what is required, yet for love's sake I prefer to appeal to you" (vv 8-9). His real concern is expressed a few lines later: "I preferred to do nothing without your consent in order that your goodness might *not be by compulsion but of your own free will*" (v. 14). Paul is in no doubt about his own authority, and could command if he had wanted to. But he regards an order that *must* be obeyed as a form of compulsion, a limiting of the free decision that is essential for authentic growth. He will not issue a binding directive in the area of moral choice.

But was Paul prepared to practice what he preached? It should come as no surprise to find that he was quite ready to commit himself. We have an instance of that in the matter of divorce. He was quite aware of Jesus' position:

> To the married I give charge, not I but the Lord, that the wife should not be separated from her husband...and that the husband should not divorce his wife (1 Cor 7:10-11).

Yet, when faced with a situation where a pagan husband refuses to live with his christian wife, Paul expresses himself without ambiguity: "If the unbelieving partner issues a writ of divorce, then let the divorce stand" (7:17). In this instance Paul permits an absolute divorce with the consequent right of remarriage:

> Paul's decision here, then, is in flat contradiction to Jesus' prohibition of divorce (vv. 10-11). It cannot be claimed that Jesus' prohibition concerned only christian marriages, and so is inapplicable in the case of mixed marriages. Jesus issued his directive to Jews and based his argument on the intention of the Creator. His directive, therefore, is valid for all marriages. Yet Paul did not obey, thus showing that he did not understand the directive of Jesus as a binding precept. It was an important expression of the ideal, and Paul underlines its permanent value by using the present tense (v. 10a), but he refused to impose the ideal indiscriminately. The ideal embodied in Jesus' prohibition was designed to illuminate and inspire, not to be used as a stick to beat the weak and the unfortunate.[4]

Paul could well expect his fellow Christians to take responsibility for their moral decisions because he took responsibility for his own.

---

[4]Jerome Murphy-O'Connor, *1 Corinthians*, (Wilmington, DE: M. Glazier, 1979, 66).

The Legacy

The exclusive salvation-way of faith which is, in Paul's view, the way of liberation and of freedom, alerts the church to ever-threatening legalism and turns it into an "open system" in which the Spirit can work. Happily, the Spirit again and again bursts through ossified structures, makes room for the exercise of freedom and maturity, and draws the church's attention to the signs of the times. Paul is not vague; he is a supreme realist. We cannot do without him. The truth is, the tragedy is, that we have not really listened to Paul — as we have not heeded his Lord. Paul has told us that God, in Christ, has made us his children (Gal 3:26). He has told us that God has set us free (5:1). As children of God we must find the courage to stand fast in the freedom Christ has won for us. It is not enough for us to be careful not to betray our freedom through irresponsibility. We must take a stand against the "yoke of slavery," against any abuse of freedom in the world or in the church.

The encounter with the risen Jesus (Gal 1:15-16) not only transformed Saul of Tarsus but has influenced the whole of christian history. It has been possible, for christian churches, to operate without much reference to Peter. Christianity without Paul is inconceivable — though, often enough, Paul's role may be hidden. It seems, however, that Paul's legacy of freedom has not yet been fully claimed by any of the churches.

11

PAUL AND WOMEN

In chapter four it was easy to illustrate Jesus' sympathetic attitude towards women, easy to give examples of his respect for womanhood. It would seem that we have to acknowledge in Paul one who, sad to say, had not understood his Master — in this respect at any rate. In my study of the New Testament I have become more and more convinced that no one has ever understood Jesus as Paul has done; he is *the* exegete of Jesus. Must I, however, admit this blind spot? After all, it is not today or yesterday that christian women have begun to regard Paul as responsible for many of their woes. Surely he does stand out as a misogynist. Look at the evidence: "Wives, be subject to your husbands" (Col 3:18; Eph 5:22); "the women should keep silent in the churches" (1 Cor 14:34); "I permit no woman to teach or to have authority over men" (1 Tim 2:12). Pretty damning, is it not? We shall see that none of this is Paul! In respect of his allegedly negative attitude to women, Paul — rather like

Mary Magdalene — stands in need of rehabilitation. Obviously, then, I must begin by putting the lie to that misogynistic Paul.

Paul and Paul

Fourteen New Testament writings are traditionally attributed to Paul. It does not follow that he is, in fact, author of all fourteen. It was clear almost from the start that Hebrews is not his work. Today there is agreement that seven writings are certainly his: 1 Thes, 1, 2 Cor, Gal, Rom, Phil, Philemon. Of the rest, 2 Thes, Col and Eph are doubtfully his; there is scholarly consensus that the Pastorals (1, 2 Tim, Titus) are quite later than Paul. It is significant that (apart from one passage in 1 Cor), a call for the submissive obedience of women is found only in the suspect letters. Already one can begin to see why Paul's "bad" reputation may not be deserved.

The author of 1, 2 Timothy and Titus would seem not to have been an immediate disciple of Paul but a man of the second or, more likely, third christian generation. He has used the names of the well-known disciples to deal with problems of the community, or communities, of his concern. Paul is, for him, the ideal apostle. And the pastoral directives, necessary for his situation, found greater weight when they were presented as issuing from Paul. While he clearly admired Paul greatly, it does not follow that he always understood Paul. In his attitude to women he is quite un-Pauline — nowhere more so than in the violently anti-feminine polemic of 1 Timothy 2:11-14.

Anti-Feminine

> Let a woman learn in silence with all submissiveness. I permit
> no woman to teach or to have authority over men; she is to
> keep silent. For Adam was formed first, then Eve; and Adam
> was not deceived, but the woman was deceived and became a
> transgressor.
>
> (1 Tim 2:11-14)

It is a sad passage. The fact that it occurs in Scripture does
not change the extreme negativity of it nor, on the other
hand, turn it into an inflexible norm. The passage must be
read in the context of the whole New Testament — and
then it is firmly relativized. The author's reading of Genesis
is plainly tendentious. In the Genesis passage, both the man
and the woman are equally guilty; indeed, God levels his
accusation at the *man*: "Have you eaten of the tree of which I
commanded you not to eat?" (Gen 3:11). The author of 1
Timothy mirrors the misogyny of ben Sirach: "From a woman
sin had its beginning, and because of her we all die" (Sir
25:24). In no way would Paul go along with that.

"The Women Should Keep Silence"

But wait a moment. What of 1 Cor 14:34-35?

> As in all the churches of the saints, the women should keep
> silence in the churches. For they are not permitted to speak,
> but should be subordinate as even the law says.

The question is: what are these verses doing here? In
chapters 12-14 of 1 Corinthians Paul replies to the final

question raised in a letter of the Corinthians to him, one concerning the "charisms" or spiritual gifts granted to members of the community. Their variety, and the rather disturbing nature of some of these gifts, tended to cause confusion. Hence Paul intervened and clarified the situation: All these gifts come from the same spirit; they are granted in view of the good of the community; their relative importance is based on the importance of the services they render; charity stands far above the gift of speaking in tongues (*glossolalia*), a gift of which the Corinthians were inordinately proud.

It is in chapter 14 that Paul describes this rather perplexing gift. And vv 34-35 of the chapter strike a discordant note: they have nothing at all to do with the matter of tongues, the matter under discussion. Furthermore, Paul is made to contradict himself. In 11:5 he has admitted that women can and do lead prayer, and prophesy publicly, in the liturgical assemblies; now (14:34-35) he demands that women be wholly silent! These verses are suspiciously like 1 Timothy 2:11-14. They are a post-Pauline interpolation from that Pastoral milieu. They ought not to be laid at the door of Paul.

A Question of Hairstyle

We are not yet out of the wood: there remains 1 Corinthians 11:2-16. Traditionally, this passage was thought to be concerned with women's head-dress and it was urged as the reason why women ought to wear hats in church. In exegesis it was regularly taken to be a matter of women's hairstyle. In fact the text is just as much concerned with male hairstyle (11:4, 14). Paul had found, to his chagrin, that the Corinthians had a positive genius for misinterpreting any teaching of his — the two letters to the Corinthians give evidence of that. In this instance the Corinthians had taken to heart, in their own way, a statement of his (surely uttered more than once) which we find recorded in Galatians 3:28 —". . .there is no male and female, for you are all one in Christ Jesus." They had responded by sporting a unisex hairstyle! The practice upset Paul: this was not at all what he had in mind.

More than Paul's Jewish sense of propriety was in question. One may guess that he was upset by a suggestion of homosexuality or, at least, he may have felt that the Corinthian practice was open to that interpretation. His first argument against the practice is from the order of creation (11:3-9) and is based on Genesis 2:18-23. Paul has gone out of his way to make clear that he does not read the Genesis text in terms of the subordination of women. That is the point of his qualifying comment: "Nevertheless, in the Lord, woman is not independent of man nor man of woman; for as woman was made from man, so man is born of woman. And all things are from God" (11:11-12). His concern is to stress the *difference* between men and women and to assert that it is a God-willed difference. The other argument (vv 13-15) appeals to common sense. In the end, Paul has to strike an authoritarian note: "we recognize no other practice, nor do the churches of God" (11:16). The authoritarian tone is more than a little dampened by the heavy weather Paul made in vv 2-15. Much ado about nothing, it might seem.

For our concern, there is Paul's matter-of-fact acceptance of a leadership role for women in the churches (11:5).[1]

To conclude this first part, we may glance at 1 Corinthians 7 where Paul fields some Corinthian questions about marriage. In that whole chapter, two factors should be kept in mind: Paul is dealing with specifically Corinthian situations, and he does so in terms of his expectation of the imminent end of the world as we know it (vv 29-31), an expectation that obviously relativizes social relationships. Noteworthy is his unqualified recognition of the sexual equality of husband and wife in marriage (vv 3-4). And his advice to the unmarried (men and women), and to widows, not to marry (v. 8) implies that women have a choice in the matter — a blow at the patriarchal system: the authority of the *paterfamilias*.

Paul's Associates

Paul's letters are occasional writings, each addressed to a specific community and its needs. If he mentions disciples it is not too surprising that they tend to be men. Nevertheless, the number of women who figure in his letters is impressive. Most of the names crop up in the long list of Romans 16 — people in Rome to whom Paul sends greetings. Nearly always the titles given to these women, or the manner in which they are introduced, are noteworthy. Paul regularly designates his own work of evangelizing and teaching as "labor-

[1] Jerome Murphy-O'Connor, *1 Corinthians* (Wilmington, DE: M. Glazier, 1979, 104-109).

ing" or "toiling" (the Greek verb *kopiaō*); in Romans 16:6, 12 he commends the women Mary, Tryphaena, Tryphosa and Persis as those who have "worked hard in the Lord." He elsewhere acknowledges that women have worked with him as missionaries, on an equal footing: Euodia and Syntyche "who have labored side by side with me in the gospel together with Clement and the rest of my fellow workers" (Phil 4:2-4). He is concerned that these two women have an obvious disagreement and entreats them "to agree in the Lord." Clearly, their position is so important that their dissension cannot but harm the community. In Philemon vv 1-2 the "sister" Apphia stands between the "fellow worker" Philemon and the "fellow soldier" Archippus — surely meaning that she, too, is a mssionary. If the name Junia(s) (Rom 16:7) is feminine, then we have a woman designated an "apostle."

Of quite special interest are Phoebe and Prisca. The former receives a solemn and warm commendation: "I commend to you our sister Phoebe, a woman-deacon of the church of Cenchreae...for she has been a patron of many and of myself as well" (Rom 16:1-2). *Diakonos* (there is no feminine form) designates an office — Phoebe is being recommended as a teacher and a missionary of a specific church. She is also a woman of some means since she is a *prostatis*, a patron. The wife-and-husband team of Prisca (Priscilla) and Aquila are mentioned in 1 Corinthians 16:19; Romans 16:3-5; 2 Timothy 4:19; Acts 18:2-3, 26. They are fellow workers of Paul and were active in Corinth, Ephesus and Rome. Important is reference to "the church in their house." And, since Prisca is regularly named first, she seems to have been the dominant partner. The author of Colossians sends greetings to "Nympha and the church in her house" (Col 4:15). The house-church was the starting-point of a christian community. It tended to mean, in practice, that a Christian of some substance offered his or her home as the meeting-place of the christian group. Naturally, the householder in question — to that extent, at least, a "patron" — must have played a significant role in the assemblies. The householder would surely have presided at the eucharist. Where the householder was a woman (Prisca, Nympha) then it is likely that she was the one who presided.

No Male and Female

It is not surprising, in view of how Paul so matter-of-factly acknowledges the ministry of women in the christian movement of his day, that he could make his own the remarkable statement of Galatians 3:28:

> There is neither Jew nor Greek, there is neither slave nor free, there is no male and female, for you are all one in Christ Jesus.

Paul is quoting and adapting a baptismal declaration. The introduction to it reads: "You are all children of God; for as many as were baptized into Christ have put on Christ" (3:26-27). With regard to Jew and Greek, Paul was almost obsessed with a concern to abolish the religious distinction between Jew and Gentile. In contrast to the specifically Jewish rite of circumcision, he sees baptism as a rite which bonded together people from all different national and social backgrounds. He saw too, that through baptism, women might become full members of the people of God — a status that could not be theirs in a religious system marked by a rite of circumcision. Paul's attitude to slavery was less clear (cf 1 Cor 7:17-24). A factor here is the economic fact of slavery in the Roman Empire — a system which Paul could not realistically challenge. There is, though, the implication of his letter to Philemon: in sending back to his master a runaway slave, now become a Christian, he invites that master to welcome Onesimus as a "brother" (vv 15-17).

"There is no male and female" — this statement is crucial. Paul has in mind Genesis 1:27 — "male and female he created them." In Jewish tradition this was primarily understood in terms of marriage and family. He is asserting that patriarchal marriage is not what constitutes the new community in Christ. Again, this is a repudiation of inequality. Another approach would be to take the underlying Genesis 1:27 as expressing the essential unity of humanity as it comes from the creating word of God. That equality of man and woman, no longer a reality in historical and existing social patterns, will, Paul asserts, be achieved in and through Christ. And he is not maintaining only that the disruptive tensions will be finally overcome at the "second coming" of Christ; he maintains that this can and should happen *now.*[2]

The issue of Jew and Gentile was soon a non-issue — simply because the christian movement had become wholly Gentile. It was not Paul but later Christians who brought about the overthrow of slavery. The equality of women and men in the christian community has not yet become a

<hr>

[2]Carolyn Osiek, *Galatians* (Wilmington, DE: M. Glazier, 1980, 39- 42).

christian reality. The signs are that our generation is witnessing a surge which, one hopes, will issue in that desired result.

I have shown that the major reason why Paul has been regarded as a misogynist is because he was taken to be author of the Pastorals. We have seen that 1 Timothy 2:11-14 carries a decidedly anti-feminist bias. The Pastorals — those pseudo-Pauline letters of about 110 A.D. — are representative of a backlash to the disturbing prominence of women in the christian movement. Where Paul, despite his thoroughly Jewish background, was able to accept a religious role for women quite at odds with that background, it is clear that later male Christians — predominantly Gentile — had wanted to call a halt to the "rot." In fact, this development is already manifest in Colossians and Ephesians.[3] There has been a firm re-statement of the patriarchal pattern.

The passage Colossians 3:18 - 4:1 is a typical domestic code,[4] dealing with the relationship between wife and husband, children and father, and slaves and masters. In each case the onus of obedience is imposed on the subordinate second partner. Noteworthy is the elaboration of the master-slave relationship (3:32 - 4:1): the text is in favour of a propertied, slave-owning class. Significant is the almost hysterical insistence on "the Lord" (in 3:24 identified as "the Lord Jesus") throughout the passage. What has happened is

[3]It is more and more widely accepted that these are pseudo-Pauline letters, dating from a generation or more after the Apostle.

[4]The domestic code, directing moral exhortations to various members of a household, was common in Greco-Roman literature. Other New Testament examples are: Eph 5:22–6:9; 1 Pet 2:18–3:7.

that the Greco-Roman ethic of the patriarchal household has been taken and imposed on a christian community — without regard to the Paul and Jesus traditions. What has happened is that a political and social *status quo* has been brought under the aegis of the Lord Jesus. The change is rough on slaves but may not, at first, have impinged too much on free women. That will change.

The change happens in Ephesians. Here the emphasis is no longer on slave/master but on the relationship of wife and husband in patriarchal marriage (Eph 5:21-33). The shift from Colossians is eloquent. The exhortation: "Wives, be subject to your husbands, as to the Lord" (Eph 5:21) is not at all the same as: "Wives, be subject to your husbands, as is fitting in the Lord" (Col 3:18). "In the Lord" of Colossians is the element that "christianizes" a Greco-Roman domestic code; "subject...as to the Lord" of Ephesians means something different. In the Colossian situation one might still make a case for equality of wife and husband; in Ephesians that is quite ruled out. Christ/husband... church/ wife: there is no relationship between equals here.[5] And the last thing the author of Ephesians wants is any such quality. The passage had opened, innocuously: "Be subject to one another out of reverence for Christ" (5:21) — the sort of general statement that Paul could have approved. But the Ephesian author, without more ado focuses on wives. Colossians had bidden children and slaves to "obey in

---

[5]"Wives, be subject to your husbands, as to the Lord. For the husband is the head of the wife as Christ is the head of the Church, his body, and is himself its Savior. As the church is subject to Christ, so let wives also be subject in everything to their husbands" (Eph 5:22-24).

everything" (Col 3:20, 22); Ephesians extends the admonition to wives: "let wives also be subject in everything to their husbands" — an admonition copper-fastened by the parallel: "as the church is subject to Christ" (Eph 5:24). Already, in v. 22 ("be subject to your husbands, as to the Lord"), the wife's submission to her husband is set on a par with her religious submission to Christ. The inferior position of the wife — and consequently the inferior position of women — has been given christological justification.

Nor is the situation retrieved by such statements as: "Husbands, love your wives, as Christ loved the church and gave himself for her" (5:25), "husbands should love their wives as their own bodies" (v. 28), "let each of you love his wife as himself" (v. 33). For there is no gainsaying the import of the opening and closing verses: "Wives, be subject to your husbands...let the wife see that she respects her husband" (vv 22, 33). There is no longer equality in the household of the Lord.

The Pastorals

One of the most interesting features of the christian movement when one realizes that, at first, it was exclusively Jewish, is that, from the start, women participated actively in the liturgy. In contrast, 1 Timothy 2:8 sounds a sad note: "I desire that in every place the *men* should pray...." Then the text goes on to speak, condescendingly, of the "modest" adornment of women (v9) before descending to arrogance and insult: "I permit no woman to teach...Adam was not deceived, but the woman was deceived and became a transgressor" (vv 11-14). A church that has chosen this rhetoric as its model for the treatment of women, rather than follow the practice and teaching of Jesus and of Paul, deserves to reap the whirlwind.

In a wider context the author of the Pastorals has firmly reinstated the patriarchal pattern. For example: "Bid the older women to be reverent in behavior...and so to train the young women to love their husbands and children, to be sensible, chaste, domestic, and submissive to their husbands" (Titus 2:3-5). In other words: teach women to know their place! Still, the author cannot quite succeed in drawing a veil over a more active feminine role. He acknowledges a rather innocuous "order of widows" (1 Tim 5:3-16). More importantly he admits the presence of women-deacons. Then, there is the intriguing 5:1-2. Literally, it runs (with the alternative rendering of the Greek terms put in parentheses): "Do not rebuke an older man (presbyter) but admonish him as one would a father, younger men (deacons) as brothers, older women (women presbyters) as mothers, younger women (women deacons) as sisters in all propriety." On the evidence I would subscribe to the view that "the leadership of the community consists of male and female presbyters on the one hand, and male and female deacons on the other."[6] It could well be that this factor and its attendant tension might account for the intemperate language of 2:11-15. One thing is clear: the anti-feminist posture of the Pastorals has no support in the authentic writings of Paul.

[6]Elizabeth Schüssler Fiorenza, *In Memory of Her* (London: SCM, 1983, 290).

Conclusion

It would not be out of place for this conclusion to reach back beyond Paul to Jesus in view of my earlier chapter on Jesus and women and my contention that Paul has rightly followed Jesus. We might, to begin with, look to two encounters of Jesus with women which had not been noted before. The familiar relationship between Jesus and the sisters of Bethany, explicitly indicated in John 11:15, is highlighted in Luke 10:38- 41. The exasperated Martha does not hesitate to point out that it is Jesus' fault that she has been left on her own to make all the preparations. That complaint is matched by the implied rebuke of John 11:21 —"Lord, if you had been here, my brother would not have died." True, in both Luke and John, these stories have been overlaid with layers of symbolism. But there still breaks through, so refreshingly, the pained protest of Martha: "Do you not care that my sister has left me to get on with the work by myself" (Lk 10:40). And there is the eloquent declaration of John: "Now Jesus loved Martha and her sister and Lazarus" (Jn 11:5).

The Lucan and Johannine traditions point to a relationship of warm friendship between Jesus and the sisters and brother of Bethany. And both evangelists agree that the closest bond was between Jesus and the women. Paul, too, we have seen, had many women friends. The simple fact is that Jesus and Paul were not afraid of women. The sad fact is that a suspicion and fear of women soon surfaced in what became the church of Christ. Jesus and Paul will ever stand in protest against any negative attitude towards women. The feminist movement of our day alerts us to an essential feature of the christian way. There is no place for second-class citizens in the household of the Lord. Only when women achieve equality can there be a household of *God*. The author of the Pastorals had restructured the "household of God" on a patriarchal pattern. That model Jesus and Paul had repudiated. Surely Jesus and Paul must know, better than any other, what is the way of God. There is a hierarchy in the pattern of revelation. The whole of the New Testament is Scripture. But, within the New Testament, the Lord and the Apostle stand apart and above. That is the testimony of two millennia of christian history — more often, let it be said, in theory than in practice.

12

PAUL AND RELIGION

Saul of Tarsus was a Pharisee who followed whole-heartedly the religion of Torah and Temple. We have it on his own word that he lived by Torah, after the strictest pharisaic principles: "...as to righteousness under the law, blameless" (Phil 3:6). That he would have been a supporter of Temple we may accept from Luke's evidence in Acts where he has Paul declare: "I am Jew, born at Tarsus in Cilicia, but brought up in this city (Jerusalem) at the feet of Gamaliel, educated according to the strict manner of the law of our fathers" (Acts 22:3). He himself tells us that he "persecuted the church of God" (1 Cor 15:9; Gal 1:13). When we read this in company with Luke's assertion of his complicity in the death of Stephen who was lynched because of his words against the Temple (Acts 7:47-51; 8:1), we can be sure that the Temple, and all that it stood for, was sacred to Paul. Though he hailed from Tarsus and was, to that extent, a hellenist, he would not have been in sympathy with the hellenistic critique of the Temple. In short, we can be as sure as it is possible to be, that the religion of Saul was that of pharisiaic Judaism, with something of a Jerusalem colouring. Paul came to understand that the christian movement was inspired by quite other priorities.

I have insisted above that Paul remained firmly a Jew. There is the interesting passage in Acts 21:17-26 where he readily went along with James' proposal that, in answer to the accusation that he had been teaching "all the Jews who are among the Gentiles to forsake Moses" (v. 21), he should sponsor four men who were ritually completing their nazirite vow. This would involve Paul's undergoing the Temple ceremony and bearing the expenses of the sacrificial offerings. It was no problem for one who could declare: "To the Jews I became as a Jew, in order to win Jews; to those under the law I became as one under the law — though not myself under the law — that I might win those under the law" (1 Cor 9:20). Paul was a man of principle, but he was never doctrinaire. In the event, James' plan did not work (Acts 21:27-36). Likely enough, Paul was not surprised. He who had "become all things to all men" (1 Cor 9:22) must have found that it is an attitude admirable in prospect but not notably productive in practice. And, despite his readiness to make a conciliatory gesture the truth is that for Paul the Apostle "religion" had come to mean something very different from what it had meant to Saul the Pharisee.

The End of the Law

I have noted that one needs to be careful about how one thinks of the "conversion" of Paul. In no way at all had he repudiated his Jewishness. If he did come to take an antinomian stand, that is to say, came to reject Torah, that did not mean a rejection of the Hebrew Scriptures. One has only to read his letters to perceive how consistently he argues from the Scriptures. We need to understand what he means by "Torah." In Romans 8:2 Paul characterizes the Torah as "the law of sin and death" while in 7:12 he has declared that "the law is holy, and the commandment is holy and just and good." One may reconcile such seemingly contradictory statements by acknowledging that Paul had respect for the law; his quarrel was with the place it had come to hold in the lives of Jews. For the Jew the Torah (including both the written Torah and the *Halakah*, the "oral law," which adapted and advanced the demands of the written law) was the full expression of God's purpose for his people. Indeed, law and Lawgiver were practically identical. In this situation the Torah took on an absolute value, and one could concern oneself exclusively with the law (to the practical neglect of God).

One who adopted this attitude to the law, Paul came to see, was, in practice, defining himself in terms of a "thing." And one limited one's possibilities by limiting, drastically, one's field of choice: the law decided, man submitted. Furthermore, this attitude was deceptive: one relied on the law (Gal 3:10) as a means of life (3:21) whereas, in fact, one's slavish reliance on it meant death (Rom 8:2). Worst of all, guided exclusively by the law, one sought authenticity within narrow, precise limits — and found a "righteousness" that was one's own and not God's. All this goes to explain why for Paul, the Torah, though "holy and just and good" remained decidedly a "thing." It was not, nor could be, an absolute and had a merely educative value. It was a "pedagogue" (Gal 3:23-25) which guided the first faltering steps of a humankind groping for authenticity. The Christian, who looked to Christ and *imitated* him, had outgrown the need of a *paidagōgos*. For if Paul had respect for the law in itself ("holy and just and good") he was quite sure that, in the time of fulfillment, it no longer had place. And that is one reason why he came to embrace a different understanding of "religion." It was a new way, but with firm roots in his Jewish past. It may be that Luke has put it well when he has Paul declare, in his defence before the procurater Felix, "according to the Way, which they (his Jewish accusers) call a sect, I worship the God of our fathers, believing everything laid down by the law or written in the prophets" (Acts 24:14). Paul himself would not have gone along with that "everything laid down by the law"; but that he worshipped "the God of our fathers" according to the Way he would have been happy with. We shall look at some basic aspects of "the Way" as Paul understood it.

Body of Christ

After his experience on the road to Damascus, Paul found himself, as disciple of Christ, to be part of a new brotherhood and sisterhood. As a Pharisee he had been conscious of belonging to a people — that was nothing strange to him. What characterized this new people was its relation to Christ. Paul came up with his image of "Body of Christ." In applying the image to the christian movement it should be clear, from all that we know of Paul, that he has not in mind an undifferentiated "oneness." Equality of women and men in Christ does not suspend multiformity and variety.[1]

We have tended to equate the Body of Christ with the church. It is needful to be clear that, in Paul's writings, the theme of the Body developed independently of that of the church. True, in Colossians and Ephesians, the themes of "body," "head" and "church" are linked and the church is identified with the "Body of Christ." But this was a later development, and does not necessarily reflect Paul's thought. We might profitably begin to study Paul's concept of the Body by noting the realism of his view of the Eucharist. In 1 Corinthians 10:16 he asks, rhetorically, (as of something self-evident to the Christian): "The cup of blessing which we bless, is it not a participation in the blood of Christ? The bread which we break, is it not a participation in the body of Christ?" Through the eucharistic experience we become associated with Christ, and our union with him should be understood in a very realistic sense. But the eucharist is a factor we may more profitably discuss later.

"Body," for Paul, is a powerful image. In Rom 12:4-5 — "For as in one body we have many members, and all the members do not have the same function, so we, though many, are one body in Christ, and individually members of one another" — the expression "one body" means the one body *of the Lord.* Paul has in mind the real presence of the Lord which is achieved when men and women serve one another through the charisms (the passage Rom 12:3-8 has to do with charismatic gifts). In 1 Corinthians 12:12-13 (again in the context of charisms) "Christ" stands for the christian

---

[1] J. Christiaan Beker, *Paul the Apostle* (Philadelphia: Fortress, 1980, 307-315).

community: "For just as the body is one and has many members and all the members of the body, though many, are one body, so it is with Christ. For by one Spirit we are all baptized into one body." Here being *baptized into one Body* surely refers to the community into which a Christian has been initiated by baptism. This is particularly clear in 12:27 — "Now you are the body of Christ and individually members of it." The community is not an aggregate of belivers but "a body" with mutually interdependent members. It is an organic unity and therefore, necessarily, has a diversity of parts; it cannot be a monolith.

The image of the "body" throws light on Paul's understanding of community. The new mode of existence that women and men achieve in Christ is not wholly their own. It is a participation, a sharing, in which others are essential. Paradoxically, Paul's understanding of sin is a help to understanding his idea of community. Man is not only born into a disoriented society — made so by the sins of preceding generations — but he contributes to that disorder by his own sins. As a Christian he belongs to a community that is, in principle, rightly oriented to God. In fact, through the failure of individuals, sin gains an entry to this sphere which ought to be immune to its influence. The personal sins of Christians provide a bridgehead for Sin and make it that much more difficult for the other members of the community to be their true selves — hence Paul's stern attitude towards the toleration of incest (or what he would call incest) in Corinth (1 Cor 5:1-5).

In short, then, my freedom to realize my potentialities and become truly human is conditioned by the authenticity of the other members of the community. Christian freedom, and its necessary correlative of responsibility, highlights in a concrete way the interdependence of Christians on one another. But all this is in the realm of interpersonal relationships, for the great danger of a christian community is to see itself as, in some way, distinct from its members. This danger is all the more real because as a human, visible reality the christian community must of necessity be institutionally organized. Too easily the community is assumed to have a value in itself which the members are ordained to serve. Uniformity in thought and action becomes a virtue and the individual finds himself cast in a mould and his authentic development is inhibited. In truth, the *christian* community exists for the sake of the individual. And its response to God is nothing other than the response of its members.

The individual must always be conscious of the community, but must never become lost in it. What Paul demands of his converts is, paradoxically, a completely altruistic individualism. Their commitment to Christ is achieved in isolation, through the loneliest decision a person can make, the act of faith. Their growth in that commitment is to be an intensely personal development of the unique potentialities that God gives to each individual. Yet, their attention is never to focus on themselves. Their whole being must be alert to detect and to minister to the needs of others. All this is possible only to the extent that the community is a *loving* community. Otherwise, there will be selfishness on the one hand and the individual will be hampered by the institution on the other.[2]

[2]Wilfrid Harrington, *Christ and Life* (Dublin: Gill & Macmillan, 1975, 129-135).

Baptism

In Romans 6:1-11 Paul turns to union with Christ through baptism; he does so in a search for the basis of christian morality. He had set aside the law as being, at best, a signpost to conduct, offering no practical help. He had stressed that justification was by faith apart from works of law. Indeed he had just declared that where sin abounds, grace abounds much more (5:20). Is there any good reason, then, why a Christian should be good? Paul's way of meeting the difficulty is to start from a consideration of baptism as the sacrament of initiation into the christian life.

Paul was quite alert to the danger of being misunderstood; the evidence is especially clear in 1 Corinthians. Here, in Romans 6:1 he shows that he knew himself to be accused of libertinism as he indignantly rejects the proposal: "Are we to continue in sin that grace may abound?" The implication is that, since God is gracious, then we may — perhaps should — give him all the scope he wants. Paul asks: "How can we who have died to sin still live in it?" (v. 2). His point is that, because a Christian is one removed from the domain where sin rules — set free from the tyrant Sin — then, as far as sin is concerned, we are dead. Christians recognize the lordship of Christ, a lordship that demands our total dedication to him.

> Do you not know that all of us who have been baptized into Christ Jesus were baptized into his death? We were buried therefore with him by baptism into death, so that as Christ was raised from the dead by the glory of the Father, we too might walk in newness of life (6:3- 4).

For Paul, christian baptism, the initiation rite into the christian community, is also something much more. Baptism is a concrete expression of faith;[3] if faith is the acceptance of the crucified Lord, so, in effect, is baptism. "Buried with him": readily enough suggested by the rite of immersion baptism — a rich symbolism. The one to be baptized goes down into the water, as Jesus descended to the grave of death; and then rises out of the watery grave, as Jesus was raised from death. The Christian's emergence to new life is at the cost of dying to sin, as Jesus died to sin; it is achieved by the power of God, as Jesus was raised by the Father's power. Our hope — an assured hope — is that one day we *might* walk in newness of life: that, one day, we may share fully in the new life which he won. Again, in v. 5, Paul insists that we *shall* be united with Christ in his glorified life. He never forgets — or lets us forget — that, in this age, christian life is life under the cross. Jesus is our Lord, here and now, in this vale of tears.

> We know that our old self was crucified with him so that the sinful body might be destroyed, and we might no longer be enslaved to sin. For he who died is freed from sin (6:6-7).

"We know" (cf v. 9) expresses the confidence of faith. We are "crucified" with Christ when we acknowledge the Crucified One as Lord. By that faith I "die" to any self-assertiveness, or "boasting" in terms of my own achievements and merits. By the "sinful body" is meant not in any

[3]"If you confess with your lips that Jesus is Lord and believe in your heart that God raised him from the dead, you will be saved" (10:9). The "confession" would be, in a particularly solemn way, the confession made at baptism.

way "body" as distinct from "soul" — this sort of dualism was foreign to Paul. The "body" is the whole self, especially as related to other persons. It is a "sinful body" because distorted by the baleful power of sin. For one "in Christ," however, that distortion no longer operates. That is why "he who has died" has been set free from the power of sin. For the Christian this "death" leads to life: "We shall also live with him" (v. 8). Again we note *shall* live: Paul's theology of the cross will not yield to a seductive "theology of glory."

> The death he died he died to sin, once for all, but the life he lives he lives to God. So you also must consider yourselves dead to sin and alive to God in Christ Jesus (6:10-11).

What is meant by the statement: Christ died to sin? It means, simply, that Jesus died rather than sin.[4] That is why in 8:3 we read that God "by sending his own Son in the likeness of sinful flesh . . .condemned sin in the flesh." The claim of sin against Jesus failed utterly, and sin was routed. The Christian, dying to sin as Christ did, can share in that once-for-all, decisive occasion and participate in the victory: dead to sin, alive to God *in Christ Jesus*. Baptism, a sharing in the death and raising of Jesus, a rite of initiation into the community of believers, is a basis for and an inspiration towards, christian living.

---

[4] "Christ by his incarnation, became a denizen of 'the flesh' [the human condition]. Sin put in its claim. In other words, Jesus was tempted to sin, as we are all tempted, in such form as sin might take for one in his situation. But, instead of yielding, and acknowledging Sin's dominion, as we all do, he rendered a perfect obedience to God . . .Jesus, in plain terms, died rather than sin; and so his death, instead of being a sign of the victory of Sin over man's true nature, was a sign of the complete rout of Sin in a decisive engagement" (C.H. Dodd, *The Epistle of St. Paul to the Romans* (London: Collins, 1959, 109-110).

Eucharist

Apart from two passages in 1 Corinthians it might have seemed that Paul knew nothing of the Eucharist — surely a salutary reminder to us that what we have from Paul are occasional letters by no means giving his whole theology or the full content of his preaching. At any rate, 1 Corinthians 11 puts beyond doubt that the Lord's Supper was part of the earliest tradition Paul had inherited. In that chapter, and previously in 10:14-22, he shows how important it was to him.

> The cup of blessing which we bless, is it not a participation in the blood of Christ? The bread which we break, is it not a participation in the body of Christ? Because there is one loaf, we who are many are one body, for all partake of the same loaf (1 Cor 10:16-17).

In the section 10:14-22 of 1 Corinthians, Paul wants to warn the "strong," the sophisticates, of Corinth that their cavalier attitude to idolatrous practices and, especially, their easy presence at temple banquets, might not be as harmless as they imagined. His point of argument is the christian Eucharist — the christian parallel to those temple banquets. Paul takes for granted that his readers admit the identification of cup and bread with Christ. The effect of their participation in the eucharistic meal is "communion" — a common union. It is clear that the point of reference is not only Christ. Through sharing in the body and blood of Christ, believers are united with him *and* with one another. In meeting Christ in the Eucharist we meet him with his body. The sharing of many Christians in the one loaf signifies and strengthens the unity among Christians which had its beginning in baptism when we were incorporated into the body of the community of Christ.

In 1 Corinthians 11:23-26 we meet the earliest reference in the New Testament to the institution of the Eucharist. Paul solemnly passes on a tradition which, because it had reached him through an authentically christian community, had come to him from "the Lord." In fact, he is citing an established liturgical formula — likely the usage of the church of Antioch. He reminds the Corinthians of this tradition in order to correct an abuse in their celebration (11:17-22). The striking point in the passage (11:23-26) is that Paul does not think of the Eucharist and Christ's presence through it in a static way as might be suggested by the formulas: "This is..." Instead, the account is full of dynamic expressions. It is no mere making present of Christ's body and blood; it is a proclamation, and a memorial, of his death, of an event. Similarly, the cup is "the covenant in my blood," that is, an event, the making of a covenant which has lasting and definitive consequences for the life of the people who are included in the covenant.

The command to repeat the action of the Lord, "Do this..." (vv 24, 26), does not only bind the community to celebrate the Lord's Supper regularly and thus keep alive the meaning of the death of Jesus, but places upon it the obligation to proclaim the redemptive meaning of his death. "Do this in remembrance of me" (vv 24, 25) is probably meant to offset an implication of Corinthian eucharistic practice which would "remember" Jesus only as a reality of the past. Paul wants to evoke an active remembrance that would make the past present by recall of total commitment to Christ. Significantly, the "proclamation" of the Lord's death (v. 26) is in terms of eating and drinking that implies a true communion — for nothing but love, expressed in warm table-fellowship, can continue to proclaim the meaning of the death of Christ.

And, just here was the Corinthian problem. The Eucharist was celebrated in the setting of a meal. It had become fashionable for the better-off members of the community to gather beforehand and dine well on their lavish provision of food and drink. Later, when the workers and slaves turned up, the Eucharist was celebrated (vv 17-22, 33-34). In Paul's eyes this was not only a glaring abuse: it was a perversion of the whole meaning and purpose of the Lord's Supper. He had declared: "Because there is one loaf, we who are many are one body, for we all partake of the same loaf" (10:17). The Eucharist was meant to be a bond of unity: in Corinth it had been turned into a wedge between the haves and the have-nots. No wonder Paul does not commend the Corinthian practice (vv 17, 22).

Because this context is ignored, verse 29 has been regularly misinterpreted — "For any one who eats and drinks without discerning the body eats and drinks judgment upon himself." Traditionally, the verse has been urged in support of the doctrine of the "real presence" — the sin is that one fails to distinguish the Eucharist from ordinary food and drink. In point of fact, the "real presence" is not an issue; the Corinthians do believe that they are eating and drinking "the body and blood of the Lord" (v. 27). The point at issue is that what was designed to unify is being used to divide. The "body" in question in verse 27 is *the body of the community*. The Corinthian celebration is not communion.

The sacrament of the body and blood of the Lord is being abused to rend the body of Christ. There is the sin.

The Spirit of Christ

The background, and source, of Paul's Pneuma-doctrine is the Old Testament: for him the "Spirit" is essentially *ruach Yahweh*, the saving activity of God. The Spirit is personal in the sense of being a power and activity imbued with the personality of God. The difference is that, for Paul, this saving power is present and active in Christ. Throughout Paul "Spirit" or "Holy Spirit" is a flexible term which is used and adapted as the situation requires. There are two points of major importance. In the first place, the Spirit is the Spirit of Jesus. For instance, Paul can declare, "God has sent the Spirit of his Son into our hearts, saying, 'Abba! Father!'" (Gal 4:6) and "Any one who does not have the Spirit of Christ does not belong to him" (Rom 8:9). And he refers to "the help of the Spirit of Jesus Christ" (Phil 1:19). In Romans 8:14-17 it emerges that the Spirit of God is the Spirit of Jesus' own relationship with the Father. And the effect of the Spirit in the life of Christians is to turn them, progressively, into the likeness of God (2 Cor 3:18) — while in fact Jesus is the likeness of God (4:4). In other words, the mark of the Spirit is a relationship with God which makes one more like Jesus. Because of Christ, and through him, the Holy Spirit is in each Christian and in the christian community; so the Spirit can be called the Spirit of Christ.

But one must go further and admit that, for Paul, Spirit reflects the character of Christ and is the presence of Christ.

This is implicit in many passages and is clear in the declaration: "The last Adam became a life-giving Spirit" (1 Cor 15:45). From his resurrection Christ is known to us as life-giving Spirit; he is experienced as Spirit. Paul, in short, does equate the risen Christ with the Spirit who gives life. Paul's answer to the question of the relationship of Lord and Spirit was one of identity: an identity amenable to christian experience in which the Lord showed himself as Spirit, and the Spirit represented the Risen One. The risen Lord is present as Spirit and is experienced as Spirit. So it is that, for Paul, "in Christ" or "in the Spirit" are two expressions of the same experience. He does not put forward a Pneuma quite distinct from God or Christ. Rather, for him, Christ in whom is concretized the saving activity of God is, as risen Lord, present and active only through the Spirit and as Spirit.[5]

Paul is not at all interested in the metaphysical question of the relationship of God, Christ and Spirit; his interest is functional. He can pass, quite naturally, from "Spirit of God" to "Spirit of Christ." By his resurrection from the dead Christ is the risen Lord, mighty in the Spirit (Rom 1:4). To him, then, is given disposal of the Spirit, of the power of God, which he possesses so fully that he himself can be regarded as Spirit (1 Cor 15:45; 6:17; Rom 8:9-11). For, after all, if Holy Spirit is the saving power of God where, more than in the risen Lord, is that saving power present? Christ is, in truth, the "life-giving Spirit."

[5]James D.G. Dunn, *Jesus and the Spirit* (London: SCM, 1975, 318-326).

Charisms

The Spirit is all very well but John has told us: "The wind (*pneuma*) blows where it wills, and you hear the sound of it, but you do not know whence it comes or whither it goes; so it is with every one who is born of the Spirit (*Pneuma*)" (Jn 3:8). Acts, in the Cornelius story, gives a helpful clue to one way of discerning the presence of the elusive Spirit. As Peter preached to Cornelius and family, his Jewish–Christian companions were "amazed, because the gift of the Holy Spirit had been poured out even on the Gentiles" (10:45). Happily for us, Luke tells us how they could discern the presence of the Spirit: "For they heard them speaking in tongues and extolling God" (10:46). Paul was to learn that it was not quite as simple as that. He had understood that the Spirit is not much involved in *glossolalia* and that more down-to-earth gifts can be a surer criterion of the Spirit of Jesus.

The whole long section of 1 Corinthians 12:4-14:40 is, by Paul, devoted to the relative merits of the spiritual gifts. The significant and — no doubt for his readers disturbing — point of his analysis is his insistence that not only is there a variety of gifts, but there is a variety of *service* and that the gifts are, essentially, gifts of service. It is not likely that the Corinthians had regarded them in this light. Paul (12:4-11) begins by pointing out that the gifts of the Spirit are more varied than the Corinthians had imagined. Their predilection for tongues and prophecy had led to dissension and Paul is determined to stress unity. He admits that the gifts are manifold but insists that all have one and the same source —

the Spirit. He indicates three categories (gifts, service, works) — his grouping and listing are not meant to be exhaustive. The "gifts" are those of wisdom and knowledge and faith (v. 8); "service" comprises prophecy, discernment of spirits and tongues (v. 10); "working" refers to healing and miracles (vv 9-10). He will insist that the purpose of these charisms (as of any gift of the Spirit) is to "build-up the community (12:7; 14:4, 12).

It is evident that Paul is replying to a query of the Corinthians and it is not difficult to guess what they had wanted his answer to be. They valued the gift of tongues above all others. Paul does not think it enough to declare that they are mistaken: he wants them to understand why they are mistaken. Tongues is but one of a great variety of gifts — all of which, he is careful to insist, come from one and the same Spirit. And all of these gifts are for the building up of the christian community. Just as the human body is an organic structure with many members having different functions, so the Body of Christ is complex and has many Spirit-inspired ministries. No one person or no one group can function for the whole Body.

The Corinthians' question to Paul had been: which is the highest gift? Or, more precisely, it seems to have been whether prophecy or tongue-speaking is the higher gift. Paul is not content to settle the matter on this level, to set off one against the other. There is "the more excellent way" (12:31) of love, in the light of which all other gifts may be evaluated. At first sight chapter 13 of First Corinthians seems an intrusion, interrupting the natural flow of chapter 12 into chapter 14. These two chapters are concerned with gifts of the Spirit, the charisms: it might seem that chapter 13, on *agapē,* is a digression. In fact the treatment of *agapē* is vital to Paul's argument and is meant to help us to see all the charismatic gifts in proper perspective. This chapter, then, enables us to evaluate correctly the Pauline assessment of the charisms. The chapter falls naturally into three parts or strophes.

1. Charity is the christian way *par excellence* (13:1-3). Paul's worry over the Corinthian preoccupation with tongues is manifest: "If I speak in tongues of men and of angels." But here concern (as it will be in chapter 14) is not that tongues should be, in some sense, articulate; it is, rather, that they might be meaningless. Gong and cymbal by themselves are without melody and simply make noise. So, too, speaking in tongues, without love, is devoid of meaning. The sacrifice of one's goods, the sacrifice even of one's life, may be motivated by other factors than love. They could be a gauntlet flung down, a fierce gesture of independence. Paul makes the uncompromising and frightening statement that, without love, even the supreme sacrifice is worthless.

2. Love is opposed to all the childish rivalries at Corinth (13:4-7). Paul's picture has positive and negative features. When all is put in terms of him, then it is indeed true that it cannot be doubted that the life and example of Jesus Christ have inspired the positive features. When all is put in terms of him, then it is indeed true that love is patient and kind, rejoices in the right, bears all things, believes all things, hopes all things, endures all things. In Jesus the love of God has revealed itself in human form. *Agapē* is not possessive love and is much more than affection: it finds expression in action; it is a love that is all-embracing and never exclusive. The negative features reflect the behavior of the Corinthian

community. Love has no place for jealousy or boasting, arrogance or rudeness. Love does not insist on having its own way, is not irritable or resentful, it does not rejoice at wrong. Christians have been called, through love, to be servants of one another (Gal 5:13).

3. A series of declarations stresses the transience of charisms (13:8-13): prophecy and tongues will cease and knowledge will pass away. Inevitably so, because prophecy and knowledge are imperfect. They are realities of this present age; they will have no place in the age to come. Here we see things in the blur of a mirror — the cloudy ancient mirror; charismatic knowledge as such is enigmatic, imperfect. Of all the gifts of God the three that abide are faith, and hope, and love; but the greatest of them is love. This chapter 13 is no digression. Paul has made his point. He has, right in the middle of his treatment of the charisms, raised prominently the standard of love. This is the yardstick against which all the charisms must be measured. More accurately, it is the supreme gift that is the measure of all the others. By his chapter 13 Paul has paved the way for an answer to the question of the Corinthians: which spiritual gift does one prefer? And his answer is, firmly, that gift which contributes to what is fruitful and which contributes to the life of the community.

Conclusion

We have looked — rather glanced — at aspects of Paul's understanding of "religion." Body of Christ, Baptism, Eucharist, Spirit, Charisms — these themes might reasonably be reckoned as essential ingredients of Paul's understanding of his Way as a disciple of Christ. He, an Israelite, now belonged to a new community that had become more and more Gentile in composition. For him, though, it was still the Israel of God, the true olive tree (Rom 11:17-24). This new community was the Body of Christ, the community that acknowledged the crucified Jesus of Nazareth as its Lord. One was initiated into this community by baptism —a rite which symbolized that one had died to the tyrant Sin and had risen to new life with God. In the Lord's Supper one entered into communion with the Risen Lord, and shared communion with one's sisters and brothers, whether they be Jew or Gentile. And the manifold gifts of the Spirit of Jesus, shared by the members of the community, were inspired and sustained by the life of the community. More than ever, then, in view of the richness of the Pauline vision, the question stands: was the "development" marked by the Pastorals really a development?[6] Perhaps the time has come to give the religion of Paul some scope. For my part, I do not believe that Paul's "religion" has ever in christian history —not even by the Reformers — been given a chance.

[6]See chapter 14.

13

THEOLOGY OF THE CROSS

I have earlier observed that the death of Jesus could be, and has been, seriously misunderstood by Christians.[1] It is, then, of first importance to try to understand aright the position of the first theologian of a *theologia crucis*: Paul. To appreciate his view one must take into account his Jewishness. There is no doubt that Saul of Tarsus would have been wholly in sympathy with the Cephas who at Caesarea Philippi vehemently rejected the notion of a suffering messiah (Mk 8:31-33). Paul the Christian was painfully conscious of the practical near-impossibility of persuading his fellow Jews that the crucified Jesus of Nazareth was the messiah of Israel. But he had, in the first place, to work out, for himself, a theology of the cross. And he did.

No one can properly evaluate Paul's achievement without a sympathetic appreciation of the challenge which he faced. It fell to him to transform a Jewish charge levelled at

[1]See p. 75.

the implication of the shameful death of Jesus: "Cursed be every one who hangs on a tree," into a statement of God's saving purpose, "Christ redeemed us from the curse of the law, having become a curse for us" (Gal 3:13).[2] Paul is being consciously paradoxical. He uses the word "curse" because it was the basis of the opposing charge. In no way at all is he suggesting that Jesus — even as our surrogate — became, in some sense, an object of God's "anger." It will become abundantly clear that, in his view, by becoming "a curse for us" Jesus manifests at once his own love and the love of his Father and ours.

"Theology of the cross" sounds grim. Yet, theology of the cross, as preached by Paul, is positive and full of hope. That is because his starting-point is the graciousness of God — or, as he calls it, the "foolishness" of God. This foolishness of God, expressed in the cross of Jesus, shows God's commitment to humankind; he is indeed a God bent on the salvation of humankind. I have already alluded to the unfortunate "satisfaction theory" explanation of the death of Jesus.[3] Nothing could be further from the truth —certainly from the truth of Paul. And Paul's truth has to be normative for authentic Christianity.

The Power of God . . .

In chapters 1–3 of Romans Paul paints a gloomy picture indeed. The whole of humankind, Jew no less than Gentile,

[2]See p. 111.

[3]See p. 129.

is in a situation of total helplessness. He has two, closely-related, reasons for his emphasis. He is sure that salvation is God's deed: it cannot be earned; and he is sure that salvation can be ours only by means of a faith that is openness to God's gift. Here, obviously, Paul is directly in the line of Jesus. One has only to turn to the parables of The Workers in the Vineyard (Mt 20:1–16) and The Servant (Lk 17:7–10). In the one case Jesus points out that salvation is purely and simply because "God is good"; in the other he points out that our good works carry no price-tag: we do our best, and we are "unworthy servants."

At first blush this second observation does not seem terribly encouraging. In fact, Jesus' message is that we have no reason for discouragement — just the opposite. If salvation were something we could earn, then we would be in dire straits indeed. If we could *merit* salvation we should have good grounds for despair. Jesus rules out *merit*. He thinks of *recompense* — something very different. A gracious God will not overlook our giving a drink of water to one who thirsts. There is not a single decent thing we do that will escape his attention. How we, perversely, got it wrong! We had built up an image, leading to and fostering guilt-complex, of a Judge who scrutinises, mercilessly, our every deed, our every thought. Jesus tells of a loving Father who, indulgently, glows at every decent act of his child. Are we prepared to heed the "scandalous" message of Jesus?

One who took to heart that scandalous teaching was, happily, the apostle Paul. As each year goes by, as one New Testament course follows another, I become more convinced that Paul is *the* exegete of Jesus. In two thousand years of christian history no one has understood Jesus as Paul had.

And the reason is not far to seek: Paul the Jew understood Jesus the Jew. At first he, understandably, had reacted violently against this "rabbi" who had undermined Torah. He came to understand that this Jesus had pointed to the true meaning of Torah, that he was the end and the fulfillment of Torah.[4] Once he had grasped that, he became the fearless preacher of the good news of Christ. With his unerring eye he discerned that the heart of that message was the folly and scandal of the cross (cf 1 Cor 1:23). He saw the cross as a positive, gracious deed.

. . .for Salvation

What had Paul to contend with? He envisaged a human world in slavery to the tyrants *Thanatos, Hamartia,* and *Nomos* (that is, Death, Sin and Law). That he should regard Death and Sin as enemies is obvious; what is unexpected is that he considered Law too as an enemy. In fact his negative attitude to Law is an important feature of his theology. It meant that he had taken to heart the word of Jesus: "The sabbath was made for man, not man for the sabbath"(Mk 2:27) — had taken it to heart with total seriousness. This is

---

[4]"The death of Christ. . .means the termination of the law (Rom 10:4), because it initiates a new eschatological life, where God and humankind meet under new conditions. And yet the new 'access' to God (Rom 5:2) satisfies the rightful claims of the law. 'The death he died he died to sin, once for all' (Rom 6:10) means that Christ satisfied the righteous requirements of the law (Rom 8:4) as expressive of God's holy will, in order to establish a new relationship to God 'apart from the law' (Rom 3:21). . .Because Christ has opened up our new access to eternal life, Christ is both the end (*le fin*) and expiration of the law, and its fulfillment (*le but*)." — J. Christiaan Beker, *Paul the Apostle* (Philadelphia: Fortress, 1980, 186-187).

a lesson we need to re-learn. The history of Christianity has shown that women and men — women more than men — have been, often enough, slaves of religion. It is high time that traditional Christianity began to look more to the subversive teaching of Jesus and of Paul. Or is a God who cares more for persons than for institution and rank too much for us? Here is where Paul's theology confronts us.

The fact remains that our God is a *Deus humanissimus* and will not be God on any other terms. It is we who seek a God who is "just." We cannot alter the truth that our God is "not the Lord of life and death but only the living Lord of Life, who wants salvation for all men and women, and not their damnation."[5] The statement is no more than a paraphrase, by a twentieth-century theologian, of the tranquil declaration of an early second-century theologian: "God our Savior desires all to be saved" (1 Tim 2:3-4). The author of 1 Timothy does not always get Paul right; in this respect he certainly does.

The opening three chapters of Romans dramatically portray a human world estranged from God. The tyrant *Sin* had got a firm grip on *sarx* ("flesh"), the human condition of weakness. Paradoxically, this weakness is the fatal human illusion of independence, of being able to go it alone. That was the first human sin recorded in Scripture: humankind tried to snatch at the wisdom that could only be a gift from God (Gen 3:1-7). Reference to Genesis is not irrelevant because Paul explicitly refers to the Adam story (Rom 5:12-20). That striving for autonomy was disastrous because humankind cannot make it without God.

---

[5]Edward Schillebeeckx, "*God, the Living One,*" *New Blackfriars* 62 (1981), 368.

All very paternalistic — unless one knows the God Paul is talking about. He is the God of foolishness and scandal, the God whose wisdom is seen in the absurdity of the cross. Acceptance of humanness is acknowledgment of our creaturehood — acknowledgment that God is Creator and that we are creatures. Creator and creature would seem to have overtones of Master and servant — except for the character of this God of ours. He is God of power, never a God of force. He is the God who displays his power on the cross. He is the God who has called his human creatures to be his *children*. It is in face of this, and only in face of this, that God puts in his claim. And it is in face of this that a human striving for autonomy is self-defeating.

Folly and Scandal

Paul is keenly aware of the difficulty of preaching the cross. After all, Jesus had been condemned by the sanhedrin, the supreme religious authority of Judaism, and one of the charges against him was that he was a messianic pretender. If the reaction of Peter at Caesarea Philippi to a Messiah who would suffer and die was spontaneous rejection (Mk 8:31-33), how much more unacceptable for any Jew to see the Messiah in one whom God had abandoned to a shameful death? As for the non-Jew: it was asking too much to recognize a savior in that same helpless figure. When Paul declared: "we preach Christ crucified, a stumbling-block to Jews and folly to Gentiles" (1 Cor 1:23), he spoke from wry experience. He will not compromise. He wants to know nothing "except Jesus Christ and him crucified" (2:2) because it was just there he had come to recognize the power and the wisdom of God (cf 1:24). Later, the author of the Johannine Letters had to insist on faith in a Jesus "come in the flesh" (1 Jn 4:2; 2 Jn 7), had to combat a view which saw the incarnation as enough by and of itself. He insisted on the saving value of the life and death of Jesus (1 Jn 5:6-8). Paul does not have a christology of pre-existence and incarnation. If he had he would have been even more forthright in proclaming his theology of the cross. Nor does Paul view the resurrection as a "saving operation." He would see the resurrection as inherent in the cross. The resurrection showed forth that "the foolishness of God is wiser than men, and the weakness of God is stronger than men" (1 Cor 1:25). He would not draw a veil over the scandal of the cross.

Reconciliation

All very well, but a two-fold question stares us in the face: Why should the death of Jesus have the power to save? And, granted that it has, how does the saving come about? If one tries to answer the question only in terms of Jesus himself then we either bow to the incomprehensible or come up with an answer that distorts the meaning of the cross. Paul, of course, knows the right answer: "God was in Christ, reconciling the world to himself" (2 Cor 5:19). God is active on the cross; it is his work. Reconciliation is *God's* deed not ours; God "through Christ reconciled us to himself" (5:18). Once one sees the cross in this way, then the saving purpose of the cross is patent.

"Reconciliation" is the key-word. Throughout the Bible rings the anguished cry of a humankind gone astray. It is all too humanly understandable that there should be a frantic scramble to effect reconciliation with God — through cult and ritual, through scrupulous observance of law. Always there was the more enlightened recognition that reconciliation was God's deed. It is no surprise that the most moving expression of this conviction should float up from the lowest trough to which Israel had sunk. We find it in a hymn of the wretched survivors of the sixth-century Babylonian invasion huddled for prayer in the pitiful ruins of Solomon's temple:

> Restore us to thyself, O Lord
> that we may be restored! (Lamentations 5:21)

Paul is following a thoroughly Jewish tradition when he insists, without remainder, that reconciliation is God's deed. For him, of course, it is more important that he echoes the teaching of Jesus. He had come to understand that God is the one who wants to reconcile humankind to himself.

God is ever the Father of the "prodigal son" — who looks eagerly for the homecoming of the prodigal, who is ready to take off and embrace him fondly when he appears on the horizon. Thanks to a "foolish" God, reconciliation is not our achievement; it is the gift of a loving Father. On the cross God displayed himself as the unjust God. We have taken for granted that justice is a supreme human value. Too easily "justice" becomes a defence of the status quo — as, for instance, the "national security" emphasis in some Latin American countries and the "law and order" preoccupation in South Africa and Northern Ireland. Happily, our God is an *unjust* God. He is the God who is supremely concerned with the underdog.[6]

That is why Jesus rejected, categorically, the label "sinner"; why he, deliberately, went out of his way to associate with "sinners." Our God is not interested in class-distinction; he is interested in people. Jesus had put it strikingly (though we, typically, had missed the point): "See that you do not despise one of these little ones: for I tell you that in heaven their angels always behold the face of my Father who is in heaven" (Mt 18:10). In the first place, the "little ones" are the weak and vulnerable members of Matthew's christian community; by the same token they are the weak and vulnerable of humankind. The saying combines two Jewish traditions: that of a "guardian angel" accredited to humans and that of the "angels of the face," the seven "top-brass" in the angelic hierarchy, those who alone stand in the immediate presence of God. What the saying adds up to is Jesus' assertion that God has committed the "little ones" not to the care of common or garden angels but to the top brass. The thrust of the statement is independent of whether one believes in guardian angels — or believes that angels exist. The thrust of it is one alternative version of Jesus' deliberately provocative saying: "God rejoices more over one sinner who repents than over ninety-nine righteous persons who need no repentance" (Lk 15:7). Jesus makes no concession. He proclaims an outrageous God who is more concerned with the helpless than with the self-satisfied righteous. This was a God whom Saul the Pharisee had to come to terms with. And Paul encountered him in the cross of Jesus.

[6]See p. 123.

True God

The cross is God's revelation of himself. It is there that he defines himself over against all human caricatures of him. His definition of himself is a challenge to the Greek God of our western tradition. The Greek heritage of philosophy, the Roman heritage of law are precious ingredients of our civilization. What we overlook is that while Greece is home of philosophy and Rome is home of law, the home of monotheistic religion is the Semitic world. The three great monotheistic religions — Judaism, Christianity and Islam — have Semitic roots. We Christians need to be more alert than we have been to the dangers inherent in the translation of the initial Judeo-Christian tradition into a non-Semitic western culture.[7] God has suffered in the exchange. The exuberant Yahweh of the Hebrews is not recognizable in the refined god of Plato and Aristotle. It is the warm God of Israel — not the bloodless God of Greek speculation — who is the Father of our Lord Jesus Christ. It is not remotely surprising that the Greeks whom Paul encountered would view a savior on a cross as an absurdity. What is sad is that Christians have, for centuries, made do with an immutable, impassible, remote hellenistic God. That "God" cannot be found in the scandal of the cross. But, then, that "God" is not the God of Paul — nor of Jesus.

---

[7]It would be absurd to suggest that the development of theology within a hellenistic thought-world was something of a disaster; I make no such suggestion. My point is that, because the hellenistic mind seemed incapable of grasping aspects of Hebrew thought, it missed out on what we today recognize to be essential aspects of the biblical God. In Greek thought God is, somehow, constrained by his own divinity; in Hebrew thought, God is supremely free.

God, in the cross, is a radical challenge to our *hubris*, our pride. He calls in question every one of our vaunted human values. The God revealed in Jesus makes no claims for himself, he bears no titles. He is the God who is prepared to be least of all, the God who serves. He is the God who makes utter nonsense of — in a church context — our jealously-guarded ranks and titles. It is just here that traditional christology faces a dilemma. Jesus Christ is true God and true man. Logically, then, one should admit that God is one who came to serve; one has to see God on that cross. It is fair to say that traditional christology has baulked at this. Modern christology is more forthright. We meet God in the *man* Jesus of Nazareth — or we do not meet him at all. Surely, then, one must have the candour to admit that we meet our *God* on the cross. Paul, former Pharisee and all, could acknowledge that because he knew that his unpredictable Hebrew God was ready for anything. He was able to accept, and embrace, the new understanding of his God revealed in Jesus. Paul was always prepared to let God be God.

The cross does not only say much about God — it says a great deal about humankind. Its first statement is obvious: a rejection of human "wisdom" — "for the foolishness of God is wiser than men" (1 Cor 1:25). Nobody in his right senses would maintain that the christian salvation story is invention. What self-respecting human (a denizen, remember, in the first instance, not of our cynical world but of a first-century world of faith and religion) would try to market that absurd "savior" on a cross! The first Christians were *stuck* with the cross. What they discerned — and what later generations missed — was the acceptable evidence (for they were Jews) of a God who could suffer. On the evidence, I say —because however strangely he might act, they were prepared to let God be God in his way. There is no way that the Greek god could end up on a cross. Paul the Jew could accept that his God, in some mysterious but real manner, was always identified with Jesus of Nazareth, to the bitter end. It seems to me that we cannot arrive at a satisfactory theology of the cross in the context of a theology stamped by Greek metaphysics. But, when one is open to the Hebrew God who is the Father of our Lord Jesus Christ, the impossible becomes logical.

True Man

Paul had, many times, spoken of "boasting" (e.g. Rom 2:17, 23; Gal 6:13). Much of the time he thinks in terms of the Mosaic law and of works of law. The Pharisee of Jesus' parable of The Pharisee and the Tax Collector would fittingly characterize the kind of person Paul had in view (cf Lk 18:9-14). The pharisee (*not* a hypocrite!) could boast of his observance of Torah — indeed, he had gone far beyond the letter of the law. The tax collector, a "sinner," had nothing but his own sense of sinfulness. But, just as the "prodigal" had turned to his father (Lk 15:18-20), so this man had dared to come to the house of his Father. Again, the message is, very clearly, that what Jesus' God looks for is a gesture towards him, an opening. He will not force — but he yearns for the fish who will turn to his lure. He is the Fisher who does not harm his fish, does not throw them back, but harvests them for his eternal harvest. Whatever image we come up with, the plea of our gracious God remains constant: "Let me save you!"

On the cross God does not only show us who he is; he shows us what it means to be human. God's Son dramatically demonstrates the radical powerlessness of the human being. He shows that we are truly human when we accept our humanness, when we face up to the fact that we are not the masters of our fate. As Jesus was stripped of his clothes, so, too, he displays a humanness stripped of every illusion.[8] And nowhere more than there did he manifest himself as the one come to serve. On the cross Jesus manifested himself as the one who had yielded himself wholly to his God. It would appear that Mark and Luke had given, in contradictory terms, Jesus' attitude to his death at the very moment of death: "My God, my God, why have you forsaken me?" (Mk 15:34): "Father, into thy hands I commit my spirit" (Lk 23:46). The fact is, that Marcan cry of God-forsakenness carries within it the Lucan confidence. Jesus is abandoning himself to the God "who gives life to the dead and calls into existence the things that do not exist" (Rom 4:17).

The cross offers the only authentic definition of humankind: God's definition. There he, gently but firmly, reminds us of who and what we are:

> On the cross God defines man as creature not in order to crush and destroy him; God defines man as creature so that he may be with man as nothing but Creator. If man depends on himself, then he has everything to fear and his anxiety will

---

[8] "Jesus' cross is essentially directed against all religious illusions and relegates man to man's humanity" (Ernst Käsemann, *Perspectives on Paul* (Philadelphia: Fortress, 1971, 35).

eventually destroy him. On the other hand, if he depends on God, then he has nothing to fear and it is the death of Jesus which made this evident.[9]

The resurrection of Jesus is God's endorsement of the definitions of both God and man which became real on the cross. And through the presence of the Risen One the message of the cross resounds through the whole of human history.

Faith

God's work on the cross is to set us free from the tyranny of Sin. To be free of sin we must trust ourselves to God. We have seen what we are; we have seen who God is. What is asked of us is *faith*: reliance on this God. Faith is the acceptance of God's gift in Christ: the gift of himself as God *for us*. Faith is the way of freedom from sin, death and law. While we may still sin, we need no longer be slaves of sin (cf 1 Jn 2:1-2). We will experience death — but the sting of death has been drawn, for death is now the way to life (cf 1 Cor 15:55-56). We may still need law — but as our servant, not our master (cf Mk 2:27-28). By faith we are set free from "works" — from any futile striving to earn salvation. Faith brings us into the domain of God where Christ is Lord: the crucified Lord. Christ is truly my Lord when I accept the truth about God and about myself. That is the way in which

[9]John C. Dwyer, *Son of God and Son of Man*, 168. The final chapter of this book, "The Cross of Christ," is a particularly fine statement of the *theologia crucis* of Paul and Mark.

I become reconciled to God. "To call Jesus 'Lord' is to ⸲
this message about who the real God is and who the real
human being is. It is to accept a God who is really Creator
and a man who is really creature — and therefore it is to
accept freedom and peace." [10]

Paul's theology of the cross is good news indeed. It should
never be used to rationalize suffering, nor to sustain a certain
cult of suffering. For it sometimes seems that an absorption
with the suffering of Jesus, a contemplation of the "precious
wounds," is morbid, to say the least. Assuredly, this is not
what Paul is about. The cross has been used to condone
injustice and oppression: suffering is privilege and marks one
as more conformed to Christ. It is true that suffering *can* be
purifying and ennobling, but it can equally well be soul-
destroying. We have seen that the cross defines God as a
God bent on humankind and defines men and women as
children of God. Paradoxically, the cross should lead to a
lessening of the burden of human suffering. Salvation means
that we, at last, become fully human, truly children of God.
To the extent that true humanness becomes a reality in our
world, to that extent oppression and injustice will yield to
brotherhood. [11] *There* is the power of the cross. "For the word
of the cross...to us who are being saved, is the power of
God" (1 Cor 1:18).

[10]John C. Dwyer, *op. cit.*, 173.

[11]This is what is meant by "kingdom of God" or "rule of God." See p. 32.

14

THE TAMING OF PAUL

The two letters of Timothy and the letter to Titus have, since the eighteenth century, been known as the Pastoral Epistles. I Timothy and Titus are of an essentially similar literary character; the second letter to Timothy has a more personal tone than the others. All three, though, have been written by the same author. He would seem not to have been an immediate disciple of Paul but a man of the second, or it may be, third, christian generation. He had invoked the names of the well-known disciples to deal with the problem of the community, or communities, of his concern. Paul is, for him, the ideal apostle. And the pastoral directives, needful for his situation, found greater weight when they were presented as issuing from Paul. It makes sense to seek to understand the Pastorals within the ecclesiastical situation of post-apostolic times. The letters are predominantly concerned with the organization and direction of the churches which the Apostle is represented as committing to the care of Timothy and Titus.

The Pastorals differ from the Pauline letters not only on the ground of different authorship but more fundamentally because they reflect a greatly changed church. A feature of Paul's outlook is his eschatological expectation; he can contemplate the parousia of the Lord happening in his own lifetime. In Pastorals the view clearly is that the church must make adjustments for a prolonged stay in the world. This involves a preoccupation with institution and with orthodoxy. Natural enough, too, is a concern with "good citizenship." Christians are expected to be model exponents of the moral and social virtues. In this way it was hoped that they would win respect and acceptance among their contemporaries in the Roman world.

Despite the emphasis on structure, no clear structural pattern emerges — certainly no obvious hierarchical institution. Indeed, one man stands out: Paul — he is the real figure of authority. Nor, despite the concern with doctrine, is there a trace of anything like an "evolution of dogma." Instead, a clear tendency runs through the Pastorals: traditional teaching is not interpreted but is firmly inculcated as an existing and permanent norm. This is, for instance, the measure of the recurring formula, *pistos ho logos* — "the word stand firm" (1 Tim 1:15; 3:1; 4:9; 2 Tim 2:11; Titus 3:8).

Paul and Paul

Our interest is in the "Paul" who emerges and, notably, in how the Pastoral "Paul" may differ from the Paul of his own letters. The picture of the later Paul is seen especially in 2 Timothy. The Pastorals presuppose that Paul is dead. The question is: how should the church cope with that loss? One way is by sticking to "sound teaching" and to tried and true regulations. Another way is by conjuring up a provocative image of the Apostle. "The church remembers Paul and models its life on him, especially on his steadfastness during suffering. The church shows 'them,' whoever these opponents may be, that it can persevere despite the loss of Paul... We see a church which has creatively adapted the life of Paul and his teachings for its own changed circumstances."[1]

The question is: was the adaptation true to Paul or was it, in some measure, a betrayal? In Pastorals Paul is, supremely, a teacher of orthodox doctrine. More precisely, he is the master who insistently exhorts his disciples to be staunch defenders of orthodoxy. The reasons for questioning Paul's authorship of these letters are cumulative. It has long seemed to me that the most persuasive of all is Paul's patronising attitude towards "Timothy" and "Titus." We know from Paul's letters that Timothy and Titus had been his apostolic colleagues from very early days. The Pastorals purport to have been written near the close of Paul's life. His veteran colleagues would not have been pleased to find themselves addressed as mere novices. And Paul would never have so insulted them. In the Pastorals we meet a Paul who is patronising, pedantic and tiresome in his preoccupation with orthodoxy: "I urged you...not to teach any different doctrine" (1 Tim 1:3); "Command and teach these things ...take heed to yourself and to your teaching" (4:11, 16); "teach and urge these duties" (6:2); "O Timothy, guard what

---

[1]Robert J. Karris, *The Pastoral Epistles* (Wilmington, DE: M. Glazier, 1979, 5).

has been entrusted to you" (6:20); "teach what befits sound doctrine" (Titus 2:1), "follow the pattern of sound words which you have heard from me" (3 Tim 1:13); "be unfailing in patience and in teaching" (4:2).

Orthodoxy

To be fair, this concern with orthodoxy is an answer to what is perceived as a real danger, and a danger within the community itself. There are Christians who do not respect the solid traditional doctrine and who propagate false views. At least, such is the author's verdict on their theology. As usual in polemic, christian charity is the first victim. (Let us recall that Paul himself had little time for judaizers). At any rate, in the author's estimation these theological rivals are self-appointed — and self-opinionated — teachers, giving themselves the airs of deeply religious men, who win introduction into private homes and, apparently without much difficulty, win over to their view certain of the less enlightened faithful; women were particularly susceptible (2 Tim 3:6-7). These false teachers are boastful, controversialists tirelessly debating pseudo-problems (1 Tim 1:4), mentally undisciplined, superficial, busy only with futile matters (1 Tim 6:4; Titus 3:9; 2 Tim 2:23), with fables and genealogies (1 Tim 1:4; 4:7; Titus 1:14; 3:9). Besides, they are self-interested, venal (Titus 1:11), seeing in religion a "good thing." (1 Tim 6:5). Hypercritical, disobedient, it can be said that they have made shipwreck of the faith (1 Tim 1:19).

There is a depth of feeling here. Who are these "false teachers"? We learn that the preaching of the adversaries is the occasion of disputes on the subject of the Mosaic law (Titus 3:9; 1 Tim 1:7); these false teachers distinguish between clean and unclean foods (1 Tim 4:3; Titus 1:15); their teaching is nothing other than "Jewish fables" (Titus 1:14). Titus is put on his guard against the "circumcision party" (Titus 1:10-11). It appears, then, that the false teachers are Jews — or, rather, judaizers, since they seem to come from within the community. On the other hand, there are some recognisable Gnostic tendencies: extreme asceticism and a negative attitude to marriage following a repudiation of worldly and bodily values.

Do Not Rock the Boat

In Chapter Eleven above we have noted, in the Pastorals, a marked hardening in the attitude toward women — a return to patriarchal standards. Not surprisingly the retrogression is even more marked in the attitude to slaves. We need to be sympathetic towards Christians trying to make their way in a world (the Roman Empire) where slavery was not only taken for granted but was a pillar of the imperial economy. It is understandable that Christians (a powerless minority) could not effectively challenge the institution of slavery. Nevertheless, it is depressing to read, in Christian documents:

> Let all who are under the yoke of slavery regard their masters as worthy of all honor, so that the name of God and the

teaching may not be defamed. Those who have believing masters must not be disrespectful on the ground that they are brethren; rather they must serve all the better. (1 Tim 6:1-2)

Bid slaves to be submissive to their masters and to give satisfaction in every respect; they are not to be refractory, nor to pilfer, but to show entire and true fidelity, so that in everything they may adorn the doctrine of God our Savior. (Titus 2:9-10).

"So that the name of God and the teaching may not be defamed"..."So that in everything they may adorn the doctrine of God our Savior." Good slaves vindicate the glory of God and the soundness of christian teaching! Good slaves witness to the saving love of God! What a betrayal of the teaching of Jesus and Paul. But the reason for it is pathetically clear: we good Christians must not rock the boat. If our neighbours accept slavery, then *our* slaves must be model slaves!

Paul was not fool enough to challenge, head-on, the Roman institution of slavery. But his attitude to slavery is quite in the line of his Master. Recall the perspective of 1 Cor 7: "the form of this world is passing away" (v. 31). The End is around the corner, so it makes very good sense that "every one should remain in the state in which he was called" (v. 20). All the more striking then, is his exhortation: "Were you a slave when called? Never mind. But if you can gain your freedom, avail yourself of the opportunity... you were bought with a price, do not become slaves of men" (vv. 21-23).

Most eloquent is the little letter to Philemon: There Paul, "an old man and prisoner for Jesus Chist" (Phm 9), writes to Philemon on behalf of Onesimus — a runaway slave of

Philemon who had found refuge with Paul and had become a Christian. Paul is sending him back to his christian master — sending home "my child, Onesimus, whose father I have become" (v. 10). And he invites Philemon to receive him "no longer as a slave but more than a slave, as a beloved brother" (v. 16). Paul knew that there is "neither slave nor free" (Gal 3:28): he has repudiated slavery. But, if the world is near its end, as he believed, why make a fuss of present inequality and injustice? Still, he could and did make that thinly-veiled request to Philemon. The author of Pastorals looked to an ongoing world, the kind of world in which we live, and asked that Christians should be good citizens. The question is, is the label of "good citizen" too high a price to pay for the passive acceptance of institutes and structures that are, in simple fact, sinful?

Back to Patriarchy

In the Pastorals, if the church is "the household of God" (1 Tim 3:15), it is a "family" clearly understood in terms of the patriarchal household. The "overseer" (bishop) should be a good *paterfamilias*, one able to manage his own household well (1 Tim 3:2-7); and the deacons, also, must be men who "manage their children and their households well" (3:12). The same is, equivalently, demanded of elders (Titus 1:5-6). Just as in the patriarchal household, wife, children and slaves must be submissive, so in the "household of the Lord," the "ordinary Christians" must subject themselves to the leaders. For that matter, submission reaches beyond the community. Titus is to remind his charges "to be submissive to rulers and authorities, to be obedient, to be ready for any honest work" (Titus 3:1). An undoubted value of this situation for the author of the Pastorals is that Christians will be seen as good citizens. But there is more to it than that — especially when one takes into account his negative attitude towards leadership roles for women:

> The Pastoral epistles advocate the patriarchal order of submission for more than apologetic reasons however. The Christian community, as the household of God, has become stratified according to the age/gender divisions of the patriarchal household. Ministry and leadership are dependent upon age/gender qualifications, not primarily upon one's spiritual or organizational resources or giftedness.[2]

The Pastorals present a church coming to terms with life: an eminently sensible church, concentrating on structure, orthodoxy and respectability. It is a sort of church with which we are familiar because, historically, the christian church followed the Pastoral model. Yet, the more one studies Paul, the more one is unhappy with the Pastorals. "That the word of God may not be discredited...so that the name of God and the teaching may not be defamed" (Titus 2:5; 1 Tim 6:1) are scarcely the most challenging motivation for christian living! There is a preoccupation with institution and office. There is an orthodoxy-fixation: "guard the deposit!" Over all this is the questionable invocation of Paul — a Paul who, most certainly, would not fit comfortably (or not fit at all), into the church of the Pastorals.

---

[2]Elizabeth Schüssler Fiorenza, *In Memory of Her*, 289.

The Real Paul

In fairness, there are echoes, in the Pastorals, of the real Paul. For that matter, there is one superlative passage, one which the Apostle would be happy to call his own:

> When the goodness and loving kindness of God our Savior appeared, he saved us, not because of deeds done by us in righteousness, but in virtue of his own mercy, by the washing of regeneration and renewal in the Holy Spirit, which he poured out upon us richly through Jesus Christ our Savior, so that we might be justified by his grace and become heirs in hope of eternal life. (Titus 3:4-7).

There is the Pauline God. A Savior who is full of goodness and loving kindness, a God who saved us, not in view of works but in his own graciousness and through Jesus Christ our *Savior* — and has made us his children and his heirs.

As for Paul himself, where he had written of his hope: "forgetting what lies behind and straining forward to what lies ahead, I press on toward the goal for the prize of the upward call of God in Christ Jesus" (Phil 3:13-14), the author of 2 Timothy, in the utter confidence that his hero, whose desire had been "to depart and be with Christ" (Phil 1:23), was now, indeed, with Christ forever, could pen his epitaph — the epitaph of the greatest Christian of all:

> I have fought the good fight, I have finished the race, I have kept the faith. (2 Tim 4:7)

One would have loved to have heard Paul's response because, when all is said and done, he could never be at home in that Pastoral church. It is clear that he had more sympathy with the turbulent Corinthians than with the Galatians and their security blanket of law. He would have found even less scope for freedom and responsibility in the Pastoral patriarchal household of the Lord.

For Freedom . . .

One may ask how Paul might feel in the Church of our day. It seems to me that foremost among our "Pauls" are the theologians of liberation. The "Pastoral theologians" are those who stress "orthodoxy" and structure and authority. The Pastoral pattern had prevailed from the second century — though never without challenge. Then came Vatican II with its liberating Pauline ethos: "For freedom Christ has set us free" (Gal 5:1). Today, the "Pastorals" are fighting back. But one feels assured that "Paul" will prevail. John XXIII opened windows that will not be slammed shut against the wind of the Spirit.